FAMILY
aroun
STRATFORD
and
BANBURY

Gordon Ottewell

Scarthin Books, Cromford, Derbyshire 1992.

FAMILY WALKS
around STRATFORD and BANBURY

Family Walks Series
General Editor: Norman Taylor

———————

THE COUNTRY CODE
Enjoy the countryside and respect its life and work
Guard against all risk of fire
Fasten all gates
Keep your dogs under close control
Keep to public paths across farmland
Use gates and stiles to cross fences, hedges and walls
Leave livestock, crops and machinery alone
Take your litter home
Help to keep all water clean
Protect wildlife, plants and trees
Take special care on country roads
Make no unnecessary noise

———————

Published 1992

Phototypesetting, printing by Higham Press Ltd., Shirland, Derbyshire

ISBN 0 907758 49 5.

NAPTON FROM THE OXFORD CANAL (Route 3)

1

Dedication

To Margaret Robson, friend and country-lover

Preface

Little did I realise, enjoying a walking holiday in the Warwickshire-Oxfordshire borderland country many years ago, that destiny would one day bring me to this lovely region of England to live.

Progress - that hateful word - has impinged on this fair landscape since then but for those willing and able to leave the bustling roads and strike off along the footpaths and bridleways, much of the old magic remains.

I have derived immense enjoyment from walking these routes, knowing that families following in my footsteps will do so, too. A few are old favourites - tried, tested and walked countless times. On others I have broken new ground and been amazed at what I had previously missed.

This rich and varied countryside awaits you. Walk in it, delight in it, and return - again and again - for more!

Acknowledgements

I should like to thank the staffs of the libraries and tourist information centres both in Warwickshire and Oxfordshire for all their patience, help and cheerfulness in the face of my many demands on their time and expertise.

Once again I have to thank my wife, Margaret, for her help and encouragement throughout.

a   b   c

a, b, c, HAZEL NUTS OPENED BY
a) Grey Squirrel   b) Wood Mouse   c) Vole

CONTENTS

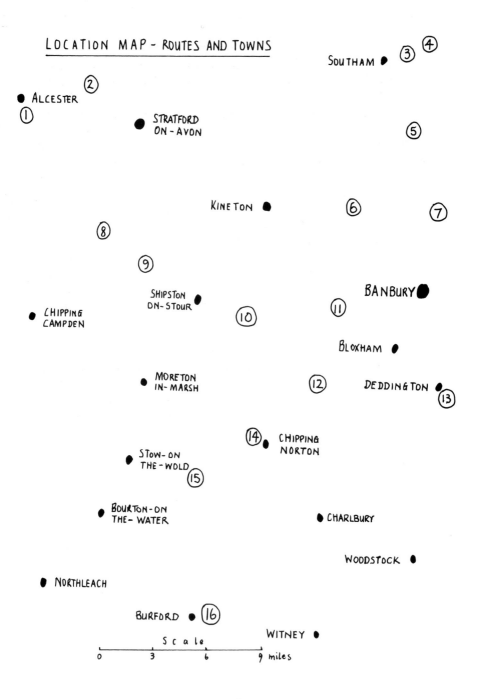

LOCATION MAP - ROUTES AND TOWNS

● ALCESTER
① ②

SOUTHAM ● ③ ④

⑤

● STRATFORD ON-AVON

KINETON ● ⑥ ⑦

⑧

⑨

SHIPSTON ON-STOUR ● ⑩ ⑪ BANBURY●

● CHIPPING CAMPDEN

BLOXHAM ●

MORETON IN-MARSH ● ⑫ DEDDINGTON ● ⑬

⑭ ● CHIPPING NORTON

STOW-ON THE-WOLD ● ⑮

BOURTON-ON THE-WATER ● ● CHARLBURY

WOODSTOCK ●

● NORTHLEACH

BURFORD ● ⑯

WITNEY ●

Scale

0   3   6   9 miles

4

Introduction

This book is intended to help families with young children to explore the countryside of South Warwickshire and North Oxfordshire in the only true way - on foot.

In order to achieve this, the book contains sixteen short walks, varying in length from 3 to just over 6 miles and ranging over the band of rural Midlands landscape stretching from Alcester and Southam in the north, southwards to the Windrush Valley near Burford, and from the Cotswold borderland of Ilmington Downs in the west, across towards Banbury and the Cherwell Valley in the east.

Just as the lengths of the walks vary, so inevitably do the demands made on the walkers. This is because the region covered is a mixture of hills, valleys, and comparatively flat country, each with its own distinctive appeal. As the chief aim is to encourage children to enjoy the open air, the routes are planned with their interests and stamina in mind. Often, there is a pub or teashop roughly midway along the route and whenever possible the more strenuous sections of the walk are tackled near the start. Road walking and retracing of steps are kept to an absolute minimum.

Under the heading 'Attractions', attention is drawn to some of the features along the route that are likely to appeal to children. Boredom-induced tiredness seldom arises if youngsters are interested and actively involved in what they are being asked to do and an unusual sighting, a snippet of colourful history, or a legend related at an appropriate point on the route can often help to revive flagging spirits and enthusiasm.

Choosing a walk

Unless the children taking part are experienced walkers, it is advisable to choose fairly easy walks first. The appendix at the end of the book lists the walks in order of difficulty and reference to this will help to avoid the mistake of making excessive demands on children's keenness and stamina. In any case, children will relish the anticipation of tackling more strenuous walks later. With very young children, it may be best to walk part of the route to begin with, or to arrange for the party to be picked up at some point on the route.

Allowing sufficient time

Each walk is intended as the best part of a day's outing, allowing time for play, exploring, and rest stops. It is better to over-estimate rather than under-estimate the time required; there is nothing worse than having to route-march the last stages of the walk. As a rough guide, allow a pace of around a mile per hour for very young children, graduating to two miles per hour for the experienced ten-year-old.

What to wear

Our notorious climate being what it is, it is advisable to go walking prepared for the worst! Sturdy, comfortable shoes are preferable to wellies, which can tire and chafe. Waterproof outer-garments, such as cagoules, are essential, while underneath, several layers of thin jumpers are better than one thick garment, as they allow more flexibility when weather conditions change. Headgear -caps and bobble-hats - should not be overlooked. And don't forget a roomy rucksack in which to carry food and drink, spare clothes, maps, guides, and so on.

Finding - and following - the way

Almost all the walking in the book is along well-waymarked public footpaths and bridleways and with careful reference to both route directions and accompanying sketchmaps, there is little danger of getting lost! Even so, it is a good idea to take along the Ordnance Survey Landranger sheet referred to under the heading 'Start', above the route directions for each walk. The routes can be found on 4 sheets - 150 (Worcester and Malverns), 151 (Stratford-on-Avon), 163 (Cheltenham and Cirencester area) and 164 (Oxford). Occasionally, especially after a summer's growth, some stiles become overgrown and stretches of footpath and canal towpaths are obscured or even partially blocked. At such times, a stout walking stick can be useful to clear the way. Farming operations, too, can result in paths being ploughed up or in other ways being made difficult to find or follow. With the growing public interest in walking and in access to the countryside generally, most farmers do their best to keep the paths clear. Remember though, that this is an intensively-farmed part of England, with arable farming accounting for much of the land-use. By law, a farmer has 14 days in which to make good a footpath after ploughing it up and county councils are taking steps to implement this requirement. If the worst comes to the worst, and the path is impossible to follow, take the shortest detour round the edge of the field to regain the route. If - although this is extremely unlikely - a footpath is wired off or in any other way deliberately blocked, make careful note of its position and report the matter to the Rights-of-Way Officer at the relevant county council office (See appendix). The presence of a bull on or near a public-right-of-way can be disconcerting to walkers. The law allows farmers to graze young bulls, and those defined as not belonging to one of the recognized dairy breeds, on or near paths, providing that they are accompanied by cows or heifers.

Refreshments

Although there is at least one pub along all but one of the routes, and most admit children, there is no guarantee that meals are provided. Remember too, that opening hours vary and some pubs are closed (for meals at least) on one day of the week. Family picnics involve some carrying - (lighter after the meal!) - but win hands-down for flexibility, economy and fun!

Public transport

Although it is assumed that most families will travel by car, the starts of some of the walks can be reached by bus or train. Helpful information on public transport is therefore included in the appendix.

About the author

Gordon Ottewell was a colliery surveyor in his native Derbyshire before becoming a teacher. He was a Primary Head in Oxfordshire and Gloucestershire until his recent retirement. Countryside exploration has been his lifelong passion and he leads walking tours in the Cotswolds, where he now lives, both for Denman College and for American walking groups. He also lectures on a range of rural subjects and is a regular contributor to 'Cotswold Life' magazine and to the 'Gloucestershire Echo'.

His books include:
Family Walks in the Cotswolds (Scarthin Books)
Family Walks in South Gloucestershire (Scarthin Books)
Family Walks in Hereford & Worcester (Scarthin Books)
Theme Walks in Gloucestershire (Thornhill Press)
Wildlife Walks in the North Cotswolds (Thornhill Press)
Gloucestershire Countryside (Minton & Minton)
A Cotswold Country Diary (Barn Owl Books).

DUCKS' DINNER, BLEDINGTON

Symbols used on route maps

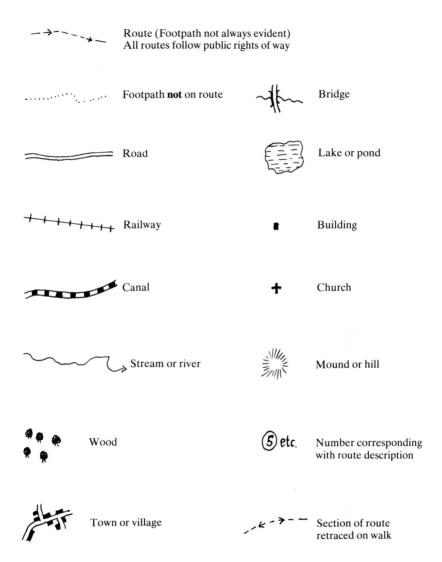

Route (Footpath not always evident)
All routes follow public rights of way

Footpath **not** on route

Bridge

Road

Lake or pond

Railway

Building

Canal

Church

Stream or river

Mound or hill

Wood

⑤ etc. Number corresponding
with route description

Town or village

Section of route
retraced on walk

WIXFORD CHURCH

Route 1   5¼ miles
Alcester and the Arrow Valley

Outline   Oversley Green, Alcester ~ Primrose Hill ~ Wixford ~ Ryknild Street ~ Oversley Green.

Summary   This is a pleasant easy walk from the edge of the little market town of Alcester over clear well-surfaced tracks to Wixford, a village with plenty of colourful historical associations. The return route follows the old Roman Ryknild Street, here merely a grassy track, before tracing the course of the River Arrow back to the start.

Attractions   As its name suggests, the town of Alcester was a Roman settlement, built at the junction of two roads, one of which, Ryknild Street, features in the walk. Also joining near the town are two rivers, the Alne and the Arrow, the latter giving its name to a village close to the route.

Alcester's long history is reflected by its mixture of old mellow-brick buildings, some of which, with timber frames, date from Tudor times. Many of the street-names are distinctive - Bleachfield Street, for instance, got its name through the rise of the linen industry in the 13th century, while the numerous old inns witnessed the expansion of the town during the early 19th century, when it became a staging post on the London-to-Holyhead coaching route.

Near the start of the walk, between Oversley Green and Primrose Hill, the route crosses the modern bypass. Notice the horse-mounting blocks specially provided for the use of riders crossing the bridge. The Heart of England Way signs refer to the long-distance footpath, here on its route from Chipping Campden in the north Cotswolds to Cannock Chase in Staffordshire.

Oversley Castle has long since disappeared, although a more recent house stands close by the mound on which it was perched. Among the variety of colourful trees lining the way down to Wixford, notice in spring and early summer the vivid yellow blossom of the laburnums. The pods, however, are poisonous, so be warned!

Wixford church is almost hidden from view at the foot of the slope. Among the trees helping to obscure it is a marvellous yew, said to be one of the oldest in Warwickshire. Notice how many of the long outer branches have had to be supported. This tree was considered a veteran as long ago as 1669, and when the rector at that time decided to have it cut down, the villagers successfully appealed to the bishop to protect their ancient tree.

continued on page 14

11

Route 1

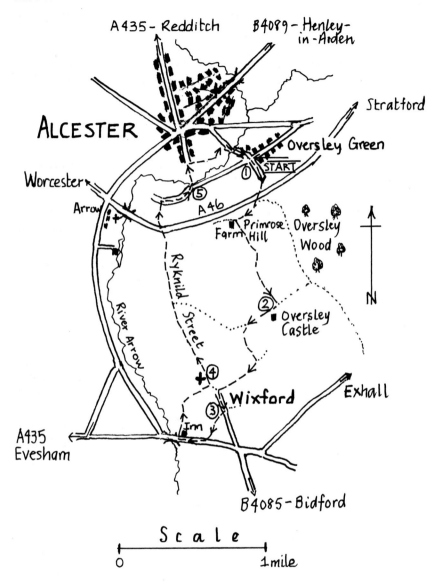

Route 1
Alcester and the Arrow Valley

5¼ miles

START *Oversley Green, Alcester, signposted from the town centre.
Park along old Stratford Road, just beyond Arrow Bridge. (O.S.
Landranger Sheet 150, G.R.096570).*

ROUTE

1. *Walk down Mill Lane (No through road) and turn left along Primrose
   Lane. Cross the A46 by the footbridge, follow the Heart of England
   Way arrow over a stile and go right, up a concrete road towards
   Primrose Hill Farm. Just before reaching the buildings, turn left along a
   wide track which winds through fields before eventually climbing to a
   junction of routes below Oversley Castle.*

2. *Turn right here and left at the next junction. At the entrance to Oversley
   Castle, bear right and go down between ornamental gate posts to reach a
   minor road near Wixford church, visited later on the walk. Turn left
   along this road and continue as far as a footpath on the right.*

3. *Turn right over a stile and cross a field to reach the B4085 over another
   stile. Cross this road to the pavement and turn right. Walk through the
   village, then cross over to the Fish Inn. The route passes through the inn
   car park and continues as a footpath through a caravan park before
   crossing two stiles and skirting industrial premises to reach Wixford
   church.*

4. *From the church, turn left along the track signposted Oversley Farm
   House, beyond which the route continues for over a mile along the line
   of Roman Ryknild Street, this stretch of which is merely a bridleway.
   Beyond a handgate, cross the A46 with care and keep right through
   another handgate to reach a minor road. Turn right along it, passing
   caravans on the left, to reach a waymarked footpath on the left, just
   before a bend to the right.*

5. *Follow this footpath, which leads to a footbridge over the River Arrow.
   On reaching a street of houses with allotments on the right, those
   wishing to explore Alcester at this stage should keep straight on into the
   town. The route continues over a stile on the right, beyond which 2 more
   stiles lead to the river bank. From here, follow a yellow arrow between a
   football pitch and a hedge to meet a road. Turn right along it crossing
   Arrow Bridge once more to reach Oversley Green and the start.*

Not far from this yew is a small thatched building, said to have been built about 300 years ago as a stable for the rector, who had to ride between Wixford and the neighbouring village of Exhall to conduct services.

From Wixford church, the route follows a stretch of Ryknild Street, the Roman road that once linked the Fosse Way, near Bourton-on-the-Water, with Watling Street, at Wall, near Lichfield, beyond which it continued beyond Derby into south Yorkshire. Between Wixford and Alcester, however, all that remains of the old road is a wide grassy bridleway, lined with old oaks and rich in wild flowers and bird life throughout spring and summer.

Refreshments Fish Inn, Wixford.

MARY ARDEN'S HOUSE

Route 2

Wilmcote and the Stratford Canal

Outline   Wilmcote ~ Newnham ~ Stratford Canal ~ Wilmcote.

Summary   An easy short walk over fields from the village of Wilmcote northwards to the hamlet of Newnham and back along the towpath of the Stratford-on-Avon Canal, a scenic waterway winding its way through pastoral countryside. The towpath walk can be extended for an indefinite distance either northwards towards Wootton Wawen from (4) or southwards from the bridge on the edge of Wilmcote to see the locks near Stratford.

Attractions   The village of Wilmcote is known the world over as the home of Mary Arden, William Shakespeare's mother. Her former house, now open to the public, is visited every year by thousands of literary pilgrims, anxious to soak up as many of the Bard's associations as possible.

Dating from the 16th century, the house is a beautiful half-timbered structure which, together with its associated farm buildings and the implements and artifacts they contain, provide us with a striking impression of what life was like in rural Warwickshire through bygone centuries up to the present day.

Modern Wilmcote, though not on a main road, is quite a bustling place. New houses jostle for space with older properties, tourist traffic ebbs and flows, and the canal, with its pleasure craft, brings extra visitors.

Newnham, reached over the fields along well-waymarked footpaths, is by contrast a quiet place today but this was not always so. There were extensive quarries near the village in Tudor times, which supplied stone for the building of Clopton Bridge at Stratford-on-Avon and for the rebuilding of St. Mary's church at Warwick after its destruction by fire in 1694. Visiting Newnham today, it is hard to realise that it once had a population of over 300 people when its quarries were in their heyday.

The year 1816 was an important one for the people of Stratford and Wilmcote for in that year the so-called Stratford-on-Avon Canal was opened. Although it had only a short life as a working waterway - it was bought by a railway company in 1856 - during this time it carried vast quantities of coal from the Midlands collieries, as well as stone from the local quarries.

Like so many canals however, it was allowed to fall into ruin from the 1880s onwards and by 1945, the section covered on this walk was unusable. In the 1960s, a valiant effort was made to restore the canal for

continued on page 18

B   15

Route 2

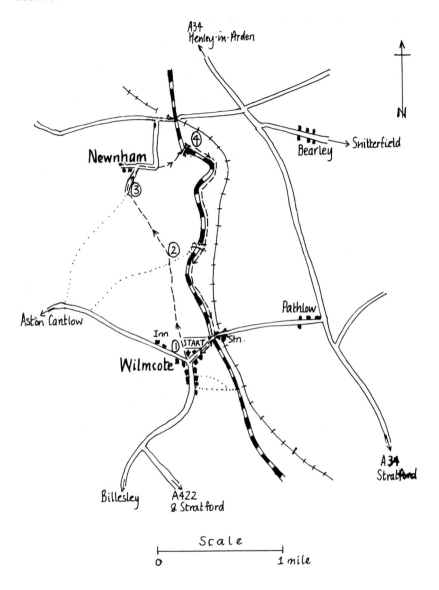

Route 2

Wilmcote and the Stratford Canal   3¾ miles

START   *Wilmcote village, 3 miles N.E. of Stratford-on-Avon. The village can be reached along minor roads from either the A422 or the A3400. Park as near as possible to the crossroads in the centre of the village, from which the walk begins. (O.S. Landranger Sheet 151. G.R.164582).*

ROUTE

1. *Follow the direction indicated by the waymark sign (yellow arrow) opposite the post office. The public footpath passes behind Mary Arden's House, between a hedge and the boundary fence. Cross two stiles and follow the hedge on the right. After crossing two more stiles, the path, which is well marked by white arrows, keeps an intermittent tree-lined hedge on the left over a long field. Cross a bridleway (indicated by a blue arrow on a gate on the left), just beyond which the route veers to the left.*

2. *Keep on along this obvious line over 4 stiles, still with hedges on the left, before eventually crossing a small field to reach a grassy lane over a stile by a gate.*

3. *Turn right along the lane, passing Retreat Farm, to reach a road. The small village of Newnham lies to the left. The route continues to the right as far as a sharp left-hand bend. Leave the road here, taking the left-hand of two waymarked footpaths (i.e. over a stile by a gate). Cross a field to a stile in a paddock fence, leaving the paddock via another stile at the overgrown junction of two hedges. Go through the right-hand hedge and swing to the left, following the hedge on the left, before climbing right along the field edge for a short distance to reach the canal towpath over a metal bridge.*

4. *Turn right along the towpath and follow it the two miles or so back to the edge of Wilmcote, which is reached by climbing up to the road at the first concrete bridge and following the pavement to the right past Mary Arden's House to the crossroads and the start.*

use as a recreational amenity and on July 11th 1964, the official re-opening was carried out by the Queen Mother.

Today, the winding canal towpath makes a delightful walk, with flowers, birds and insects to enjoy, together with quaint iron bridges spanning the 'cut' at intervals, split in the centre to allow tow-ropes to pass through.

Refreshments   The Masons' Arms, Wilmcote.

NAPTON WINDMILL

Route 3   3 miles
Round about Napton-on-the-Hill

Outline   Napton village ~ Windmill ~ Oxford Canal ~ Chapel Green ~
Napton.

Summary   A short easy walk around the interesting village of Napton-
on-the-Hill, routed along footpaths, lanes, a canal towpath, and minor
roads. For those requiring a more challenging walk, this can be linked
with Route 4, to give an 8½-mile walk providing an absorbing experience
for those families especially keen on canal-towpath walking.

Attractions   As its name implies, Napton-on-the-Hill stands high - an
unusual setting for a Warwickshire village outside the Cotswold region.
There was a village here at the time of the Domesday Book, grouped
around the hilltop, 500 feet above sea level, and it prospered to such a
degree that by the Middle Ages, it had become a town of about a
thousand people with a weekly market and an annual three-day fair. For
some reason, Napton declined in later years from being one of the biggest
towns in the county to the large village we see today. The hill, of course,
has always played an important part in its history. Its quarries yielded
stone for building, it provided an ideal site for windmills, and it gave rise
to a legend concerning the church.
  According to this legend, the villagers in the 12th century, having
decided to build a church, chose a spot near to the site of the present
green and carted loads of stone there ready to begin work. However,
under the cover of darkness, fairies carried the stone up to the top of the
hill, finally persuading the villagers that this lofty site would be the best
place, after all. Legendary fairies were of course, far removed from the
delicate, dainty-winged creatures so often portrayed in later books!
  Napton windmill, now a private house, is a striking landmark for
miles around. The present mill, though old, may have replaced other
mills that once crowned this breezy hilltop. Apparently, at one time two
mills stood side by side, giving rise to the story that the sails of one were
removed because there was not enough wind to drive both!
  From the footpath below the mill can be seen several huge ironstone
boulders wedged into the hillside. At the foot of the hill, a new industrial
estate occupies the site of the old Napton Brick and Tile Works that once
gave employment to generations of village people. This works was
conveniently situated alongside the Oxford Canal and boatloads of bricks
and tiles, marked with Napton's own windmill-motif stamp, were shipped
continued on page 22

continued on page 22

19

Route 3

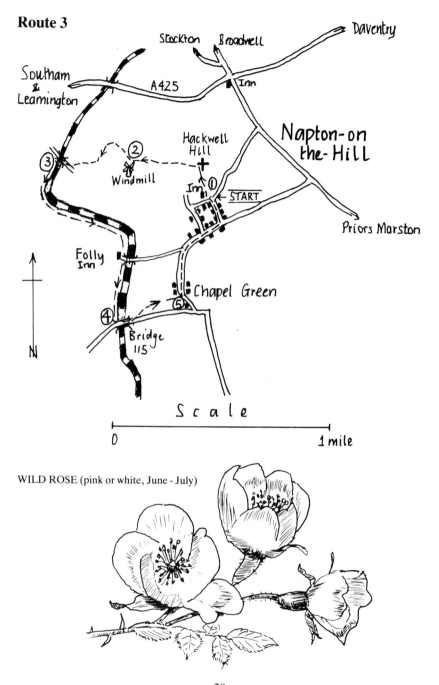

WILD ROSE (pink or white, June - July)

Route 3

Round about Napton-on-the-Hill   3 miles

START *Napton-on-the-Hill, a village just south of the A425 (Leamington-Daventry road) 4 miles east of Southam. Park in the centre of the village, near to the Crown Inn, from which point the walk begins. (O.S. Landranger Sheet 151. G.R.464612).*

ROUTE

1. *Facing the Crown Inn, climb the metalled path to the right. Cross the road signposted School Hill to reach the church, perched high on Hackwell Hill. Leave the churchyard along a path to the left of the church porch to reach a track over a stile. Turn left along it. Keep straight on. Napton windmill (now a private residence) comes into view ahead.*

2. *At the mill gate, the footpath, indicated by a yellow arrow, veers to the right and dips by old quarries. Follow the path as it swings to the right, passing great ironstone boulders, before descending to the left of an old brickworks to reach a stile to the left of a house. Turn right along a road here and, after crossing a humpbacked bridge, descend to the canal towpath.*

3. *Turn right along the towpath, keeping the canal on the left for almost 1½ miles and passing the Folly Inn, before reaching bridge 115.*

4. *Climb up to the road here and turn right. In 50 metres, turn left through a metal gate (yellow arrow) and strike off diagonally right over a field. Pass a corner of two hedged fields on the right and cross a stream by a metal cart bridge. Climb the slope ahead to reach a drive over a stile by a garage. Bear left to reach a road at Chapel Green.*

5. *Turn left along it to return to Napton. Ignore side turns. The Crown Inn is on the left.*

SKYLARK (light brown 17cm)

21

across the country. The kiln in which these bricks and tiles were made was reputed to be the largest of its kind in Europe.

Two interesting buildings passed on the closing stages of the walk are the canal-side Folly Inn and the former Methodist Chapel, now serving in the unusual role of a nickelodeon and organ museum.

Refreshments   The Crown Inn, Napton.

NEAR NAPTON

Route 4   5½ miles
Grand Union and Oxford Canals

Outline Bridge 109, Oxford Canal, Napton ~ Napton Reservoir ~ Calcutt Locks ~ Calcutt bridleway ~ Oxford Canal ~ Napton Junction ~ Bridge 109.

Summary Not just one canal, but two, feature on this route to the north of the village of Napton-on-the-Hill, around which the preceding walk was routed. Combined, the two give an 8½-mile route suitable for those families wishing to undertake a more ambitious expedition along canal towpaths. Taken on its own, this route offers plenty of variety, for in addition to the towpath sections, there is a mixture of footpath and bridleway walking as well as the novelty provided by Napton Reservoir.

Attractions Although as its name implies, Napton stands on a hill, the countryside to the north of the village is uniformly flat. However, the coming of the canals saw a new feature appear in this lowland landscape of the Warwickshire-Northamptonshire border and although canals are no longer the arteries of commerce they once were, they provide plenty to interest walkers of all ages.

It is the Napton feeder reservoir, rather than the canals themselves, that is first encountered on the walk and the natural-history interest provided by this extensive sheet of water is considerable. Mallard, coot, and great-crested grebe breed along the reedy fringes, several species of gull are regular visitors, and a heron can often be seen wading into the shallows in search of unsuspecting prey. Other birds worth keeping a watch for are the little grebe (dabchick), pied wagtail and the exotic looking kingfisher, which occasionally speeds low over the water. Aquatic insect life is dominated by the various species of dragonfly, which find the habitat provided by canals and their reservoirs ideal. The smaller, delicate species of this tribe, known as damselflies, are sometimes present in great numbers, most having predominantly blue colouring, although red and green varieties can also be identified.

Calcutt locks will appeal to those interested in canal life. Many of the brightly-painted pleasure craft seen here and elsewhere along the route have been converted from original narrow boats, which once plied the inland waterways carrying a range of freight. Ironically, the railway, which contributed to the decline of the canal trade around the Napton area, has now closed, as can be seen from the bridge and track bed between Calcutt locks and the bridleway linking the two towpath sections of the walk.

continued on page 26

23

Route 4

24

Route 4

Grand Union and Oxford Canals   5½ miles

START   *The bridge over the Oxford Canal on the Stockton-Broadwell road, ½ mile north of its junction with the A425, near Napton-on-the-Hill. From Leamington and Southam, turn left just beyond the King's Head Inn. Ignore a left turn and park on the roadside verge near the bridge. (O.S. Landranger Sheet 151. G.R.463623).*

ROUTE

1. *Take the waymarked footpath alongside the rubble road to Wigrams. Cross three fields diagonally over stiles to reach Napton Reservoir. Turn left along the embankment. Cross a footbridge to reach the towpath of the Grand Union Canal. Turn left along it to Calcutt locks. Cross two plank bridges and a lock (Care needed) and keep left along the towpath. After about a mile of towpath-walking, and immediately beyond a red-brick bridge, turn right through a gap in the hedge to reach a road.*

2. *Follow the road to the right. Eventually, this road swings right over a railway bridge and then left, to end at a gate. Continue along a bridleway (blue arrow) and keep a hedge on the right through 4 fields. On entering a 5th field, keep straight on to reach a farm road. Follow it down to a gate and continue, ignoring a right turn and with Lower Shuckburgh church spire straight ahead, until it swings left towards a farm. Continue straight on here, up the slope ahead before descending to the towpath of the Oxford Canal.*

3. *Turn right along the towpath (which can be eroded and overgrown in places). On reaching the junction of the Oxford with the Grand Union, in just over a mile, cross the humpbacked bridge.*

4. *Keep straight on as far as the next bridge (number 109). Climb up to the road at this point, back to the start.*

It is not until the last mile of the route that the junction of the Grand Union with the older Oxford Canal is reached. This link, which puts Napton firmly on the canal map, was also responsible for the loss of trade, and therefore importance, of the Oxford Canal, which as can be seen on Routes (5) and (7), was allowed to retain the winding, contour-controlled route chosen by its designer, the canal pioneer, James Brindley.

Refreshments The King's Head and the Crown Inn, Napton.

17th CENTURY GATEHOUSE, WORMLEIGHTON

Route 5

Wormleighton and the Oxford Canal

Outline Wormleighton ~ old village site ~ Oxford Canal ~ Wormleighton.

Summary This short walk explores a delightful little village, passes the
site of its predecessor, and after following the towpath of an early canal,
climbs back to the village once more. As with other canal-side walks
described in this book, keen walkers can extend the route in either
direction, providing that they are prepared to retrace their steps or enjoy
the challenge of planning alternative return routes with the help of the
Ordnance Survey map.

Attractions It would be hard to find a quieter village than
Wormleighton, yet the place has had more than its share of upheaval over
the centuries. The trim estate cottages, set in spacious gardens, reveal
little of the turbulent past. Even the splendid gatehouse, built in 1613 and
emblazoned with the coat of arms of the Spencer family, is recent
compared with the remains of the old village, nestling between modern
Wormleighton and the Oxford Canal. Here, until plague, famine and
sheep enclosures combined to hasten its end, stood a village with its
streets, cottages and manor house, complete with fishponds, surrounded
by narrow boundary banks. What remained of this village - called 'The
Old Towne' on a map of 1634 displayed in the church - was demolished by
William Cope, a prosperous sheep farmer, leaving the scatter of mounds
we see today. The Civil War, too, made its mark on Wormleighton. The
'new' manor house, used by King Charles's nephew, Prince Rupert, as his
headquarters before the Battle of Edgehill, was destroyed by the
Royalists to avoid it falling into the hands of Cromwell's forces and what
we see today is merely a fragment of what must have been a splendid
building.

Then, in 1778, Wormleighton witnessed yet another far-reaching
event, which was to change the appearance of the local landscape for
ever. This was the cutting of the Oxford Canal, one of the earliest to be
constructed in what is now called the 'Canal Craze' period. The man
responsible was James Brindley, who believed in taking his canals in wide
curves, rather than in spending time and money in tunnelling through
hills.

Walking alongside Brindley's canals is never dull. Every curve
presents a fresh aspect of the landscape and it is easy to forget that the
canal is a man-made, rather than a natural feature, for it seems as much

continued on page 30

Route 5

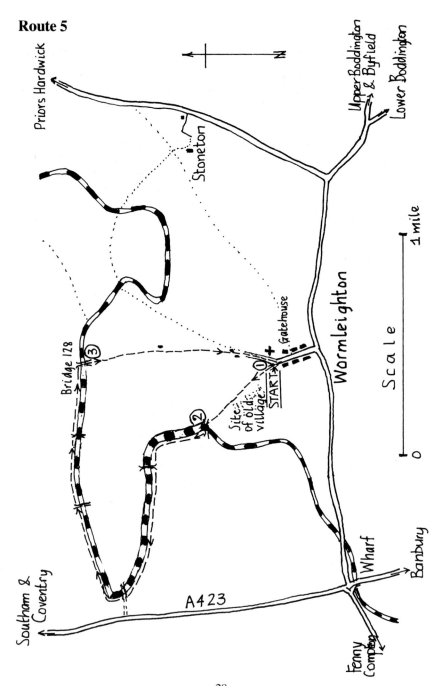

Route 5
Round about Wormleighton 3½ miles

START   *Wormleighton. The village lies on the Fenny Compton-Byfield road, 1½ miles east of the A423 (Banbury-Southam road). Park in the village. (O.S. Landranger Sheet 151. G.R.448537).*

ROUTE

1. *Walk through the village, passing under the gatehouse, dated 1613. Opposite the church, leave the road along a concreted track which dips to the left. At the bottom, by a sewage farm, go through a handgate on the right and climb the bank into a field. Make for the humpbacked canal bridge visible ahead. The route passes the old village site on the left. Go through a handgate and after crossing the bridge, descend to the towpath.*

2. *Turn left. The route keeps the canal on the right for about 2½ miles, as far as bridge 128.*

3. *At this point, leave the towpath to follow a bridleway on the right, which climbs steadily from the bridge through fields, back to Wormleighton. At the top of the slope, it swings to the right between barns, to emerge in the village. The church is on the left.*

LAPWING (glossy black & white 30cm)

part of the scene as the hills, rivers and woods. This short stretch of towpath-walking passes some interesting bridges, one of which appears to have been made from the trunk of a single tree. Unfortunately, the towpath is badly eroded in places and care is needed. Otherwise, the combination of scenery, wild life and peace makes for happy family walking.

Refreshments The nearest pubs are at Fenny Compton and Priors Hardwick.

POND ON WARMINGTON GREEN

Warmington, Ratley and Hornton

Outline Warmington ~ Ratley ~ Thompkins Barn ~ Hornton ~ Warmington.

Summary This is a walk in the Edge Hill area of Warwickshire, taking in two attractive Warwickshire villages and an Oxfordshire one. The route is a mixture of climbs and descents, none of them extreme, chiefly along footpaths and bridleways. However, encroachment from crops and intrusive wild growth in late summer can make walking difficult in places, so families are recommended to concentrate on a few of the easier walks before tackling this one.

Attractions Many people consider Warmington, from which this walk begins, to be the prettiest village in Warwickshire. Grouped around a large and well-kept green, the yellowish-brown stone houses certainly make a memorable sight and it is easy to see why artists are drawn here to try to capture the 'chocolate box' effect of the place during the summer months.

Somehow, it seems appropriate that such an immaculately-kept village green should be graced by an equally formalized pond. This is the home of a number of ducks which, although well-preened and suitably decorative, seem determined to lower the tone of the place as they waddle after visitors, raucously clamouring to be fed.

Although the route skirts the next village, Ratley, it is well worth making a short diversion to see. This is a high village on Warwickshire standards, and there is a rugged attractiveness about its clutter of ochre-stone cottages, all at different heights and angles. In 1642, the Battle of Edgehill, the first clash of arms in the Civil War, took place about two miles to the north-west and it is said that many of the dead were buried in a mass grave in the churchyard. Naturally enough, stories of ghosts are told in and around the village, including one of sightings of a young man galloping over the slopes on a white charger, and reputed to be King Charles's nephew, Prince Rupert.

Hornton, the last of this trio of interesting villages, is one of those places - Collyweston, Stonesfield and Taynton are others -famous for miles around for their building stone. 'Hornton stone' is not all quarried at Hornton itself but it is distinguished by its rich colouring, ranging from ochre to greyish-brown. Nowhere is this ochre tinge seen to better effect than in the buildings of Hornton village, where the thatched roofs,

continued on page 34

C 31

Route 6

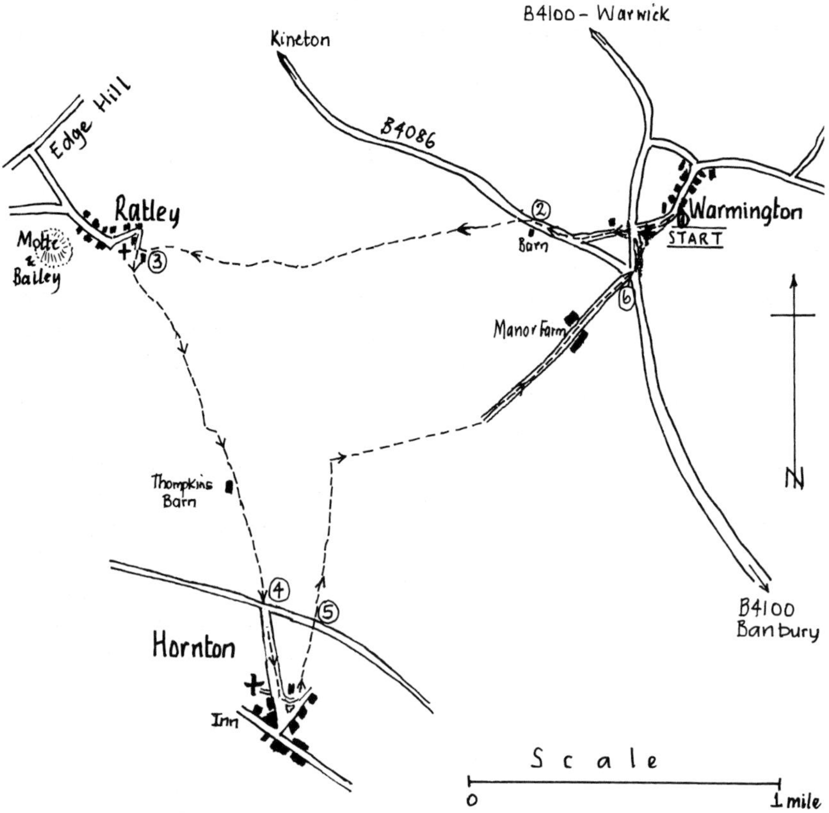

Kineton

B4100 - Warwick

B4086

Edge Hill

Ratley

Warmington

START

Motte & Bailey

③

Barn

②

Manor Farm

⑥

B4100
Banbury

Thompkins
Barn

Hornton

④

⑤

Inn

N

S c a l e

0   1 mile

WEASEL

Route 6

Warmington, Ratley and Hornton 5½ miles

START *Warmington, a village ¼ mile east of the junction of the B4100
and the B4086, 6 miles N.W. of Banbury. Park in the village. (O.S.
Landranger Sheet 151. G.R.413477).*

ROUTE

1. *Walk up the village street past the church to reach the B4100. Cross this
busy road with care and, immediately opposite the junction, climb the
bank up a zig-zag path to reach a road. Follow this to the B4086. Turn
right and, after passing a barn on the left and just before reaching a
power line crossing the road, turn left over a stile.*

2. *Keep a hedge on the right for about 70 metres to another stile. Cross and
descend a field past the left-hand of two power poles to another stile.
Cross a field and enter a second through a hedge gap. After passing a
solitary oak, the route reaches a track by a gate. Turn left and follow the
track to its end at 2 field gates. Go through the left-hand one and climb a
field, aiming for the top power pole. Climb a hunting jump by a white
gate (yellow arrow) and keep a power line on the left. Descend a field,
cross a stile and climb to another stile in a fence to reach a farm road.
Turn left and descend down to Ratley.*

3. *At the foot of the slope, the route turns left to follow the track past
Featherbow House (village straight ahead). Approximately 100 metres
along the track, go over a stone stile on the right and walk the length of a
long field to a stile by a gate (yellow arrow). Cross the next field along
the same line to a handgate by a ditch. The route now follows a shady
path, crosses a stream, and passes through a handgate. Follow a hedge
on the left up a field as far as a metal gate to join a track. This soon
swings to the right and joins another coming in from the left. Pass
through Thompkins Barn farm and follow the track to meet a road.*

4. *Cross the road and descend to Hornton, a village well worth exploring.
From beyond the phone box at the foot of the slope, the route turns
sharp left up Eastgate and then left again to follow the waymarked path
between Cromwells and Pear Tree Cottage. Cross a stile into a private
garden and continue through a delightful dell to a handgate opening into
a small field. Go over a stile at the top left-hand corner and bear right to
follow a paddock fence. Go through the fence ahead to reach the road
once more.*

5. *Go straight across and along the track (bridleway) and follow it the 1¾ miles to its junction with the B4100. The route dips to cross a stream before climbing to go through a gate and pass farm buildings, by which time it is well surfaced.*
6. *Cross the B4100 and bear left along the pavement to reach a public footpath alongside Warmington churchyard. This keeps the churchyard wall on the left and descends a flight of steps to join the outward route near the start of the walk.*

---

mullioned windows and fine proportions of the houses create a most pleasing effect.

Older children with a sense of the macabre will relish a chance to see the medieval 'Doom' painting above the chancel arch in the church. This depicts in graphic detail the dead rising from their graves and is amazingly well preserved, considering that it was painted over 600 years ago.

Refreshments   The Dun Cow, Hornton.

LOCK-KEEPER'S HOUSE, CROPREDY

Cropredy, Wardington and the Oxford Canal

Outline Cropredy ~ Oxford Canal ~ Wardington ~ Upper Wardington ~ Broadmoor Bridge ~ Oxford Canal ~ Cropredy.

Summary   This is a walk in the upper reaches of a Thames tributary, the River Cherwell, from Cropredy, through the gentle rolling north Oxfordshire country close to Northamptonshire. The route follows footpaths, bridleways, minor roads, and finally, a canal towpath, to arrive back at Cropredy, a quiet enough place today but with a few touching reminders of its brief involvement in the Civil War.

Attractions   The village of Cropredy is a watery place. It stands on the west bank of the River Cherwell, here only a modest-sized stream, despite having received the waters of the Highfurlong Brook near the start of the walk. There are also several smaller streams contributing their share round about.

But it was the coming of the Oxford Canal in the 1780s that gave Cropredy the watery appearance we see today. James Brindley took his waterway between the villages and the Cherwell, spanning it with three bridges, all of which lie on the route. In addition, a lock, together with a lock-keeper's house, was constructed not far from the centre of the village. From being a riverside village, Cropredy became a canal village, and so it remains.

But it is as the site of a Civil War battle that Cropredy gains a place in national history. On 29th June 1644, a skirmish took place in the water meadows to the east of Cropredy bridge, resulting in the deaths of several of Cromwell's soldiers and the capture of a quantity of his artillery.

Earlier, the villagers, fearful that the rare eagle lectern in their church might fall into the hands of the Puritans, hid it in the Cherwell, where it remained for thirty years. When the precious bird was at last raised from its muddy hiding place, the villagers discovered that it had lost one of the three brass lions decorating the base of its pedestal. Keen-eyed children will soon spot its dull-coloured bronze replacement, made by a local craftsman.

Of Wardington, the other village featuring on this route, one visitor aptly wrote: 'The village straggles along the hills and loses itself in green hollows'. The finest of Wardington's buildings, the manor house, lies on the route, as do no fewer than three inns and a number of attractive old houses built in the local ochre-coloured stone. The effect is one of a warm glow, especially in spring and autumn sunshine.

continued on page 38

Route 7

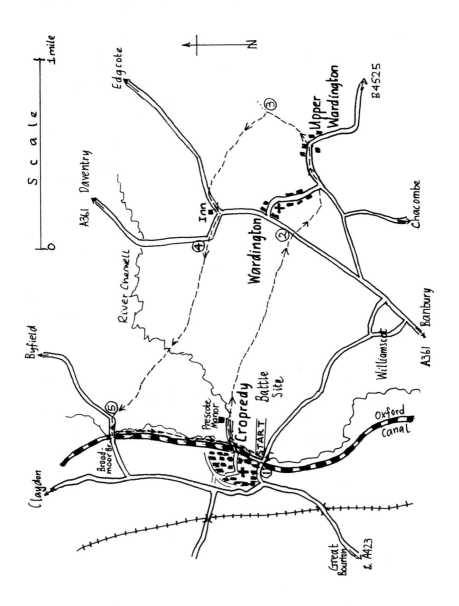

Route 7

Cropredy, Wardington and the Oxford Canal   5¼ miles

START   *Cropredy. The village lies roughly midway between the A423 and the A361, due north, and about 4 miles from Banbury. Park on the verge near a garage and stores between the canal and river bridges, on the road from Williamscot. (O.S. Landranger Sheet 151. G.R.469466).*

ROUTE

1. *From the canal bridge, descend to the towpath and turn right. On reaching the next bridge, pass under and climb up to reach a road through a handgate. Turn left, following this road past a 'No Vehicles' sign. Cross a bridge and, just before the end of the wall surrounding Prescote Manor, turn right over a gated bridge and follow the river to the left. Cross a stile in a hedge, 30 metres from the river bank. The route heads up the length of a field to a stile midway along the belt of woodland ahead (yellow arrow). On leaving the wood, continue over a field, along a course roughly parallel to a hedge on the right, to another stile. Aim now for a tree in the right-hand hedge on the brow of the next field, beyond which the route keeps the hedge on the right as far as a low stone stile at the top right-hand corner of the field. Keep the same line over the next field to a metal gate, again at the top right corner, to reach the A361.*

2. *Cross straight over the A361 and across a field to a kissing gate. Cross another field and take the left hand of two stiles 20 metres apart to enter Wardington playing field. Cross diagonally right by a pavilion to reach a crossroads by the manor house. Follow the signpost to Upper Wardington. On reaching the sloping green, dip down to follow a signposted footpath between houses. Go over a stile into a field and cross to the far left-hand corner. Go through two metal gates and climb straight up a field to a stile by a gate.*

3. *Here, instead of crossing, turn left along fenced woodland. Cross a double stile and two normal ones, keeping a boundary on the right. At a bend in the hedge by a small building, the path goes down the field diagonally to reach a road over a stile. (Note: alternatively, keep on down the field side to reach a road by another stile). Turn left, passing the Hare and Hounds inn, to reach the A361. Turn right along it (care needed - no pavement).*

37

4. *In 200 metres, where the road bends to the right, keep straight on through a metal gate. Follow a bridleway, with hedges on the right, through 5 more gates. Go through a small wood, cross the infant Cherwell and a farm track, and strike off over the next field to a gateway in a hedge. Beyond, head half-right over the crest of a sloping field and down through two gates to a road.*
5. *Turn left and continue as far as the canal at Broadmoor Bridge. From here, turn left along the towpath back to the start.*

The last stretch of the walk, along the Oxford Canal towpath from Broadmoor Bridge to the starting point, is perhaps more rewarding from a natural-history point of view than the rest of the walk. This is because unlike the intensively cultivated fields, the canal towpath and its margins consist of undisturbed habitat in which wild flowers, birds and insects are able to live out their lives in comparative safety. Get a copy of the British Waterways pamphlet 'Wildlife on the Oxford Canal' and take it with you on the walk.

Refreshments   The Red Lion, the Hare and Hounds and the Plough, all at Wardington, lie on or near the route. Other inns at Cropredy.

MEON HILL

Meon Hill

Outline   Upper Quinton ~ Coleman's Hill ~ Hidcote Combe ~ Hidcote Manor ~ Mickleton ~ Upper Quinton.

Summary   This is the longest and perhaps the most demanding walk in the book. It would have been even more strenuous but for the fact that there is no public right-of-way over the summit of Meon Hill itself, which means that we have to be content with skirting the lower slopes of this celebrated northern outlier of the Cotswolds. As befits such an upland route, the views are impressive, with plenty of historical, folk-lore and wild life interest along the way, most of which follows well-waymarked public footpaths.

Attractions   An air of mystery surrounds the solitary, steep-sided slope of Meon Hill, gazed at from afar by many but well known to very few. One writer, describing it from his viewpoint on the main Cotswold ridge, said 'Meon Hill puts out among the tree-billows like a square-rigged galleon'. Most writers, however, are fascinated by its associations with witchcraft and dark deeds generally; one well-known author, who lived close to the hill for much of her long life, wrote in her last book: 'Meon Hill has never lost its aura of mystery for me, so that when I see it I can still feel a faint thrill of apprehension'.

According to legend, the hill, like so many scattered across the country, owes its existence to the Devil. Angered at the building of an abbey at Evesham, the evil one is supposed to have hurled a giant clod of earth to destroy it. Fortunately, however, St. Egwin, Bishop of Worcester, who had founded the abbey, witnessed the wicked deed and as a result of his prayers, the clod fell to the ground and became Meon Hill.

One of the ghost stories associated with the hill concerns Christmas Eve and New Year's Eve. At these times, a huntsman and his hounds are said to chase a phantom fox around the foot of the hill. One story goes that the ghostly rider is condemned to chase his prey through eternity in punishment for hunting on the Sabbath day, while in another, the apparition is that of a huntsman who insisted on hunting by night and fell victim to his own hounds who failed to recognise him in the darkness.

Two fine gardens, both open to the public, feature on the route. Hidcote Manor (National Trust) is the creation of an American, Major Lawrence Johnston, and is really a collection of beautiful formal gardens,

continued on page 42

39

Route 8

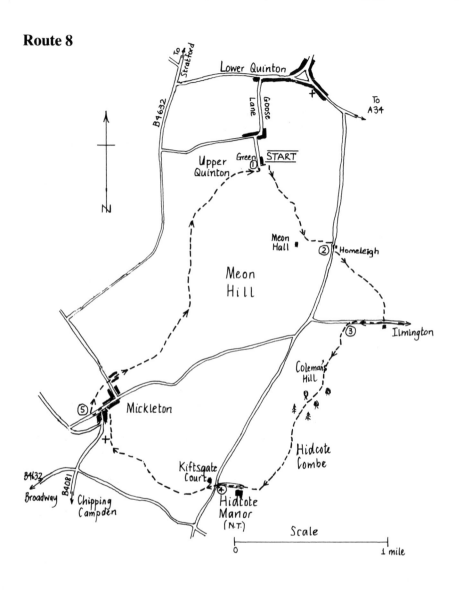

Route 8

Meon Hill

6¼ miles

START   *Upper Quinton. The village lies one mile east of the B4632, 3 miles N.E. of Mickleton and 7 miles S.S.W. of Stratford-on-Avon. Park by the green, off Goose Lane. (O.S. Landranger Sheet 151. G.R.177463).*

ROUTE

1. *Walk up the road with the 'No through road' sign. By Meon Cottage, follow the footpath on the left, signposted 'Centenary Way'. Cross two stiles before turning right alongside newly planted trees. Cross another stile and climb a field diagonally to a stile at the top left-hand corner. Keep a hedge on the right as far as a metal gate, beyond which the route crosses a field corner to another stile. Keep a hedge on the left for 70 metres. At a yellow arrow, leave the hedge and carry on over a field to a stile leading to a farm road near Meon Hall. Turn left to reach a road.*

2. *Turn right, and in 50 metres, left through a gate. Cross a long field diagonally to the right. Beyond a tiny plank bridge, the route veers right for a short distance before swinging left, with a hedge on the left, round another large field to reach a road through double gates opposite a house. Turn right along the road and in 400 metres, cross a stile on the left.*

3. *Follow yellow arrows over a footbridge, keeping a stream on the right. Cross stiles over old ridge-and-furrow and climb Coleman's Hill to enter the first of two tracts of woodland. Beyond the second, at Hidcote Combe, the route crosses parkland along a faint grassy track, climbs a stile, and keeps a hedge on the right before dipping diagonally to reach a road at Hidcote Manor (and the delightful hamlet of Hidcote Bartrim) through a metal gate. Bear right down to a T-junction.*

4. *Go through the blue gate opposite and descend to Mickleton by following the blue arrows. At the foot of the slope, ignore a stile on the left. Instead, keep on through the handgate. Follow the path, skirting the churchyard, to enter the village along a metalled path. Turn left along the B4632. In 20 metres, cross carefully to reach Back Lane and the playing field.*

5. *Instead of climbing a stile beyond the children's playground, cross the field to another at the far right-hand corner. The route now follows the Heart of England Way, crossing the B4632 and passing old glasshouses before crossing a T-junction of tracks near a small greenhouse. Beyond, the route is clearly waymarked as it skirts the western slopes of Meon Hill before dipping to cross a double stile and reaching Upper Quinton at a stile by fuel tanks. Keep on down the lane back to the start.*

walks, lawns and trees. Nearby, the privately-owned Kiftsgate Court, another fine garden set on a hillside overlooking Mickleton, has a more intimate atmosphere and offers superb views across the vale.

Mickleton, Gloucestershire's most northerly village, has an interesting mixture of Cotswold stone and timber-framed houses, as well as a playground for children.

Refreshments Hidcote Manor Gardens (admission charge). Three Ways Hotel, Mickleton.

ILMINGTON

Route 9

Ilmington Downs

Outline   Ilmington ~ Pig Lane ~ Lark Stoke ~ Ilmington.

Summary   Ilmington Downs, Warwickshire's tiny fragment of the Cotswolds, is the highest part of the county and the quality of the scenery is on a par with that around Chipping Campden and the rest of the north Cotswolds included in neighbouring Gloucestershire. The walking - along footpaths, bridleways and minor roads throughout -begins with a testing climb but the views, the wild life, and above all, the remoteness of this corner of Warwickshire, makes this a walk both to enjoy and to remember.

Attractions   The starting place for this walk, Ilmington, is essentially Cotswold in character, with sturdy stone-built houses grouped round a large green and tiny lanes wriggling off in all directions. There is a feeling of spaciousness here, enhanced by the vast contours of the Cotswold escarpment, rising away to the south and west. The village was once famous for its mummers' plays and morris dancing, the Ilmington Morris Men being especially noted for a linked-handkerchief dance called 'Maid of the Mill'. One village worthy still remembered with affection is Sam Bennett, known as 'The Last of the Troubadours' and renowned for his repertoire of ancient folk tunes, played on a 17th-century fiddle.

Fame of another kind almost came Ilmington's way some 200 years ago. At about that time, a chalybeate spring was discovered in the village and the medicinal qualities of the water were held in such high regard that but for its remoteness, Ilmington may well have developed to rival Leamington and Cheltenham as a spa.

Today, Ilmington is still the centre of one traditional rural craft. This is hurdle-making, and the craftsman's workshop, outside which a specimen hurdle is usually displayed, is passed on the return route into the village. Hurdles have been used for penning sheep since the earliest days of sheep farming. They are made both from locally-grown willow and from ash, the former being popular among shepherds because they are light to carry, while ash hurdles, being made from tougher wood, tend to last longer.

The bridleway known as Pig Lane, a scenic section of which is walked as it keeps its straight undulating course over the downs, is said to have got its name because pigs were driven along it in distant times. Such routes are often many centuries old and there is some evidence that Pig Lane is of Roman origin.

continued on page 46

43

Route 9

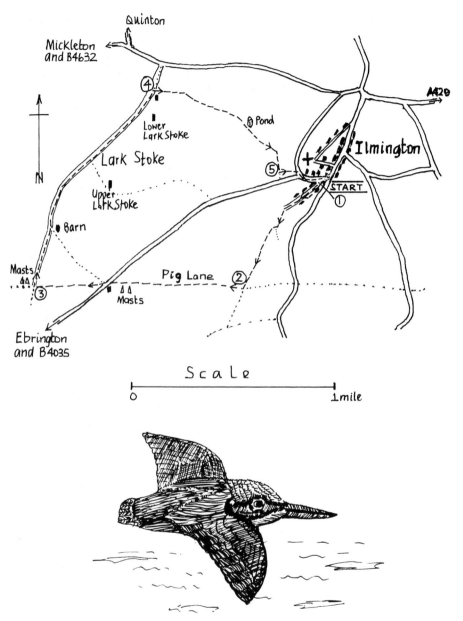

KINGFISHER (blue, red and white 16cm)

44

Route 9
Ilmington Downs

4¼ miles

START   *The village of Ilmington, 4 miles N.W. of Shipston-on-Stour and reached along minor roads from the A429. Park near the village green. The walk starts from here, at the war memorial cross by the road on the upper part of the green. (O.S. Landranger Sheet 151. G.R.211433).*

ROUTE

1. *From the road by the war memorial cross, facing the parish church, turn left along the 'No through road'. Beyond houses, this becomes a footpath. At a fork marked by two arrows, just before a gate, turn right down a bank, cross two stiles, and turn left along a fence to pass a line of willows on the left. There follows a steady climb, with a hedge on the left, up to a stile, beyond which the path continues to meet Pig Lane (a bridleway).*

2. *Turn right along this lane and follow it past two masts and down to a road. Cross and go through a handgate opposite. Climb to a second handgate at the top of a field, beyond which the route follows a wall on the right up to a minor road by two more masts.*

3. *Turn right along this road and follow it downhill for 1¼ miles, passing Lark Stoke, as far as a double entrance to a farm track on the right.*

4. *Go through a gateway (noting the Centenary Way sign) and, in 40 metres, turn left down a field edge to a stile (yellow arrow). Turn left, cross a stream, and climb a slope to a stile by a gate. Now keep a hedge on the right, crossing a stile and maintaining the same line until Ilmington comes into view ahead. Watch for a stile on the right and, after crossing it, follow the right-hand arrow diagonally across a tiny valley, with willows and a pond on the left. Climb to cross a stile by a power line post and go over ridge-and-furrow to the next stile, beyond which yet another overlooks Ilmington church. Cross and skirt a field edge to a stile at the bottom corner.*

5. *Take the left-hand path, which bends along the hedge to a gate leading into a sunken lane. Follow this to reach the village near a hurdle-maker's workshop. Turn right and then left back to the start.*

Lark Stoke, now only a couple of farms, may well have been a village long ago. The Brent family, generations of whom lived in this lonely spot, are commemorated by monuments in Ilmington church. Members of the family interested in such things may wish to play 'Hunt the Tractor' on the last stages of the walk. A number of abandoned models in various stages of decay are passed between Lark Stoke and Ilmington.

Refreshments   Howard Arms and Red Lion, Ilmington.

THE GREAT ELM OF SUTTON

Route 10   5¼ miles
Brailes Country

Outline Sutton-under-Brailes ~ New House Barn ~ Grove End ~ Upper Brailes ~ Lower Brailes ~ Sutton-under-Brailes.

Summary This walk is so called because it passes through three villages nestling under Brailes Hill, all of which owe their names to this prominent landmark. As with Meon Hill (Route 8) there is no right-of-way over the summit of the hill itself but from the stretch of the walk along the eastern flank, on either side of New House Barn, there are excellent views south-eastwards over the valley of the Sutton Brook, walked later on the route, and beyond towards the Stour Valley and the Oxfordshire border. Apart from the stretches through the three villages, most of this walk follows public footpaths. There are a few gentle climbs but nothing really strenuous.

Attractions The starting place for this walk, Sutton-under-Brailes, is one of those fortunate villages possessing an extensive green, an ideal spot both for play and relaxation. Two features worth looking out for on the green are a Victorian postbox and a giant tree stump - all that remains of the so-called Great Elm of Sutton, which towered 150 feet above the green until it crashed to its doom in 1967. Since then, the notorious Dutch-elm disease has accounted for thousands of other elms across Warwickshire and the rest of the country and those who can remember these fine trees still miss their distinctive shape. By the church gate at Sutton stands the old school, with the wheel-frame of its bell still in place. There is a text on the wall nearby, just about decipherable to keen young eyes.

The most notable feature at Upper Brailes is the castle mound, just off the route but reached by a short diversion. The 12th century castle, built by Roger de Newburgh, Earl of Warwick, has long since disappeared but with a little imagination, children will have no difficulty in storming this ancient fortress and then defending it from other intending invaders.

According to historians, Brailes - possibly Upper and Lower combined - was once a large market town with a prosperous wool trade. Certainly, the size of St. George's church at Lower Brailes suggests this, for it is a vast building, with a 120-foot high tower, completely out of proportion to the modest-sized villages it now serves.

Nature-lovers in the family will find the last stage of the walk, which follows the course of the Sutton Brook, full of interest. In particular, the

continued on page 50

Route 10

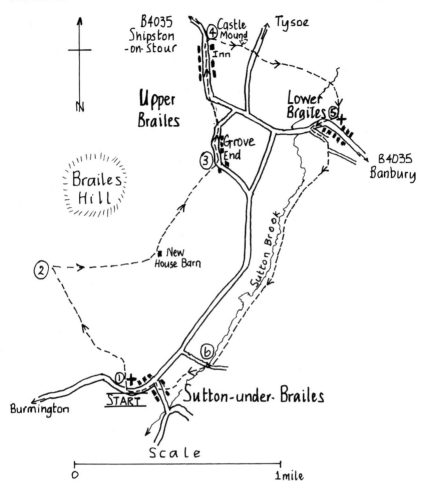

Route 10 map showing Upper Brailes, Lower Brailes, Sutton-under-Brailes and Brailes Hill, with numbered waypoints 1–6, Sutton Brook, and roads to Shipston-on-Stour (B4035), Tysoe, Banbury (B4035) and Burmington.

Route 10

Brailes Country

5¼ miles

START *Sutton-under-Brailes. The village lies midway between the A34 and the B4035, 4 miles S.E. of Shipston-on-Stour. Park by the green, as near as possible to the church. (O.S. Landranger Sheet 151. G.R.299374).*

ROUTE

1. *Cross the waymarked stile to the left of the church. A second stile leads into an orchard, beyond which a third gives access to a field. The path goes half-left to reach a farm road. Turn right along it, to reach a gate. Go through and climb a field with a fence on the left. Pass through another gate and keep a hedge on the right along a track to reach a small clump of pines at the top of a slope.*

2. *Just beyond the trees, turn right through a gate (blue arrow) and follow a bridleway skirting Brailes Hill. Keep a hedge on the right as far as New House Barn. Pass the farm on the right and go through a gate straight ahead. Keep on through another gate, following the path under trees. Eventually, it dips through a steep little hollow (wet in winter) to reach a road at Grove End.*

3. *Turn left and ignore a tempting footpath on the right. Watch for a stile on the left in ¼ mile, alongside a power pole. Cross and enter an orchard, leaving it by another stile, beyond which the route crosses a field to reach the B4035 and Upper Brailes through a kissing gate. Cross the road and turn left along the pavement, following it past the Gate Inn to reach the village allotments.*

4. *Follow the footpath sign to the right into the allotments. The castle mound is straight ahead. The path zig-zags between the plots to reach a stile by a gate. At this point, a short diversion can be made to explore the castle mound by following the hedge on the left. Resuming the route, continue to cross a road, following the yellow arrow through a large field. The path meanders in a general direction to the left of Lower Brailes church tower. Stiles lead the way over more fields until, beyond a flight of steps and a footbridge, the route swings right to reach a drive via a stile to the left of the church. Turn right to enter Lower Brailes.*

5. *On reaching the village street, turn right and soon left, along School Lane. This soon becomes a footpath. At a crossroads of paths, turn right, crossing a track via stiles to enter a large field. Aim for the far right corner, to cross a stile to the left of a footbridge over the Sutton Brook. Instead of crossing, keep the brook on the right to the corner of the next field and cross a stile in the hedge on the left. Now keep a hedge on the right as far as a farm track. Keep left along it, still following the brook. White arrows mark the route from now on, over a golf course before reaching a track over a stile.*

6. *Cross the track by the stile and, in 50 metres, go down to cross the brook by a footbridge. The path climbs a field to a stile in the hedge on the left, then crosses two more fields to reach a lane by a cottage. Turn right to return to Sutton-under-Brailes village green. The starting point is on the left.*

---

spring and summer bird life - finches, thrushes, tits and warblers - is abundant.

A new golf course has been established here recently, evidence of the current policy of farmers to put surplus land to new and profitable use as a leisure amenity for townsfolk and tourists.

Refreshments   Gate Inn, Upper Brailes. George Inn, Lower Brailes.

THE CASTLE MOUND, BRAILES (Route 10)

Around and about Swalcliffe

Outline   Swalcliffe ~ Roman road ~ Chillaway Cottages ~ Blenheim Farm ~ Great Barn ~ Swalcliffe.

Summary   This short walk explores the valley of the tiny River Swale, a tributary of the river Cherwell, beginning and ending at the village of Swalcliffe, between Brailes and Banbury. Apart from two short stretches of village-street walking, the route is entirely along a bridleway (once a Roman road) and public footpaths. Swalcliffe is a village of above-average interest. It possesses three exceptionally fine buildings - a parish church with Saxon workmanship, a rectorial manor house, and a superb great barn, dating from the early 15th century.

Attractions   Swalcliffe (pronounced Swaycliffe) is a village of the so-called ironstone belt of north Oxfordshire, as can be seen from the distinctive tawny-coloured stone from which most of the older houses are built. The oldest surviving of these can be seen down the lane below the green, opposite the church. They date from the 17th century and several have thatched roofs.

However, the Iron Age people, followed by the Romans, lived in the Swale Valley long before then and it is towards what remains of their settlements that the walk is directed. From the lane dipping towards Swalcliffe Lea, a rounded hill comes into view straight ahead. This is Madmarston Hill, on the summit of which Iron Age people constructed a defensive camp round about 200 B.C. Most of the camp has been destroyed by ploughing but aerial photographs reveal the line of the ramparts.

During the Roman period, a town grew up to the south of the hill, to be followed by Saxon and medieval settlements, all traces of which have now disappeared.

The line of the road which the Romans built to link their town with others still exists, however, although now in the form of a bridleway, sometimes known as the Salt Way, because that valuable commodity was carried along it. The route follows this road along its typically straight course for over a mile and beyond a bend in its line near Farmington Farm, before swinging left to return to Swalcliffe along the south side of the valley.

Back in the village, a visit to the newly-restored great barn sets the seal on the walk. This fine building dates from 1409 and was constructed to store the grain and other produce grown on the manor farms, which

continued on page 54

Route 11

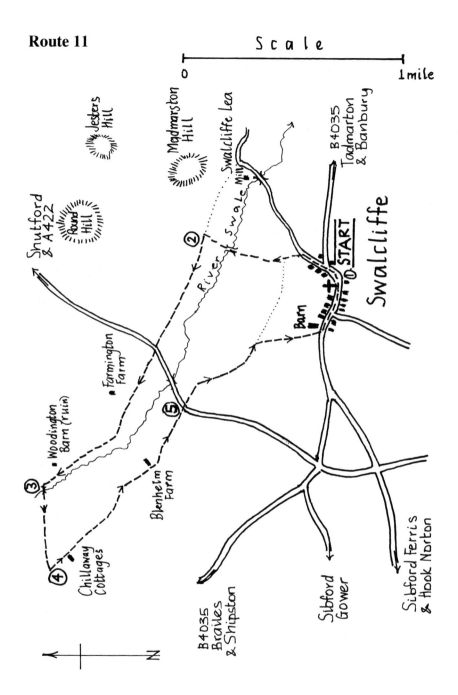

Scale

0   1mile

Jesters Hill

Madmarston Hill

Swalcliffe Lea

Swalcliffe Mill

B4035 Tadmarton & Banbury

Shutford & A422

Round Hill

River Swale

②

START ⓪

Swalcliffe

Barn

Farmington Farm

⑤

Woodington Barn (ruin)

③

Blenheim Farm

④

Chillaway Cottages

B4035 Brailes & Shipston

Sibford Gower

Sibford Ferris & Hook Norton

N

52

Route 11
Around and about Swalcliffe

4½ miles

START *Swalcliffe village, on the B4035 (Shipston-Banbury road) 8 miles west of Banbury. Park in the village, near the church. (O.S. Landranger Sheet 151. G.R.378379).*

ROUTE

1. *From the church, walk along the pavement in the direction of Banbury. At a signpost indicating 'Swalcliffe Lea. Gated road', turn left. 40 metres beyond the point at which the hedges flanking the road end, leave the road, turning left along a track. Follow this track and cross the river to reach a T-junction with another track.*

2. *This is a Roman road, now merely a track of variable width and quality of surface. Turn left along it and follow it for almost 1½ miles, crossing first a road, then a small stream at a handgate, before eventually passing through a wide gateway with the ruined Woodington Barn on the right. Just beyond a power pole, and before reaching another wide gateway, veer to the left to go through a gate and cross a stream by a footbridge.*

3. *From this bridge, climb the field ahead to reach a tree-lined hedge and keeping this on the left, follow it up to the top corner of the field. Go through a gate, keeping the hedge on the right. Beyond the next gate, follow a hedge on the left for 40 metres to reach a farm road through another gate. Turn left here and follow this road towards Chillaway Farm Cottages.*

4. *Keep to the left of the cottages down to a handgate (blue arrow). With a hedge on the right, proceed to the next gate. Beyond, turn right up the field side for 100 metres before swinging left to follow the bridleway towards Blenheim Farm. On reaching a farm road, follow it past the buildings (ignoring an old signpost serving in a decorative role on the left!) as far as a road.*

5. *Cross the road to pass through a handgate. Swalcliffe church can now be seen straight ahead. After crossing a field, go over a footbridge and another field to meet a farm track. Keep left along this track as far as a hedge, climbing the sloping field on the right. Turn right here along the hedge side, passing a tree clump on the left, before passing between bushes to reach the B4035 once more. Turn left into the village, past the Great Barn on the left, to reach the start of the walk.*

53

belonged to New College, Oxford. It is 120 feet long and like other old buildings nearby, it has walls of local ironstone, together with sturdy oak timbers. Notice the tall porches, through which loaded wagons entered, and the stone floor, on which the crop was threshed with flails and later winnowed to separate the grain from the husks.

Families wishing to learn more about the barn, and about the village, should get copies of the two informative leaflets on Swalcliffe, which can be obtained from Banbury Tourist Information Centre or in the village.

Refreshments   Stag Inn, Swalcliffe.

THE CASTLE MOUND, SWERFORD

Swerford and Hook Norton

Outline Swerford ~ Cradle Barn ~ Cradle Farm ~ Park Farm ~ Hook Norton ~ Old Railway Nature Reserve ~ Swerford.

Summary This walk takes in two contrasting north Oxfordshire villages on either side of the little River Swere, in the switchback country between Banbury and Chipping Norton. A walk of contrasts, chiefly along public footpaths, and with plenty of historical and wild life interest, it has something to offer for every taste.

Attractions Over 40 years ago, one writer described Swerford as 'One of the friendliest of the brown villages, with many ups and downs, wooded gullies, and choppy hills'. The place has changed little today. Scrambling up to the top of the castle mound, it is hard to imagine that conflict of any kind could have taken place here -perhaps it didn't, for the castle itself disappeared centuries ago, leaving precious little evidence, either recorded or on the ground, of its existence. In fact, we know more about the cottage we pass at the foot of the castle field - a datestone tells us that it was built in 1691 and apparently it was once an inn called the Griffin.

Hook Norton, by contrast, is a big, bustling village, where industries of several kinds have come, and in some cases, gone, leaving plenty of traces to look out for. The most prominent of the departed industries is the railway. The pillars of the viaduct that carried the Cheltenham-Kings Sutton line dominate the scene. This line once carried processed iron ore from a local works to South Wales. After closure in 1965, the section of line including the viaduct became a nature reserve and an informative notice about the varied wildlife population can be seen at (5).

Another departed industry that has left a few traces in Hook Norton is cloth weaving. This was carried out in the village cottages during the boom in the Cotswold wool trade and the characteristic long upper windows, necessary to provide plenty of light for the weavers, can still be seen in some of the cottages.

An industry that continues to thrive in Hook Norton is brewing, and the brewery, a strange tall building somewhat resembling a Chinese pagoda, is worth searching for at Scotland End, at the north-west corner of the village. The speciality is known as 'Old Hookey' and thirsty parents may wish to sample it at one of the village pubs.

continued on page 58

Route 12

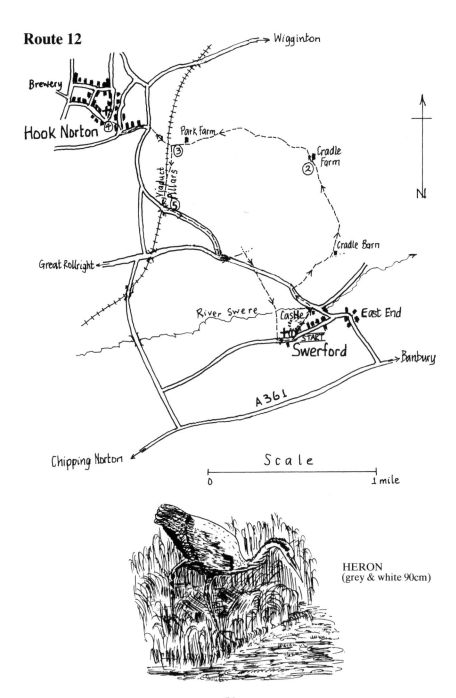

Wigginton

Brewery

Hook Norton ④

Park Farm ←

③

Cradle Farm ②

Viaduct Pillars ⑤

Cradle Barn

Great Rollright ←

River Swere

Castle

START

Swerford

East End

Banbury →

A361

Chipping Norton ←

S c a l e

0   1 mile

HERON
(grey & white 90cm)

Route 12

Swerford and Hook Norton   5 miles

START   *Church End, Swerford village. Swerford lies half a mile north of the A361 (Chipping Norton-Banbury road) and is approached along a minor road one mile west of the junction with the B4022. Park by the green, near the church. (O.S. Landranger Sheet 151. G.R.372311).*
ROUTE

1. *With the church on the left, walk along the road for a short way, as far as a lane on the left. At the foot of the slope, at the motte and bailey sign, cross a stile to see the castle remains. Descend the irregular field towards a cottage at the bottom right-hand corner and cross a stile to reach a road. Turn left, passing ornamental gates, and climb as far as a sign indicating uneven road ahead. Go through the metal gate opposite this sign and follow the stony track to reach a metalled drive (bridleway) at Cradle Barn. Keep left along it, almost to the entrance to Cradle Farm.*

2. *50 metres before the farm, turn left through a handgate in the hedge. Keep straight on with a fence on the left to reach another handgate on the right at the corner of the field. Continue down a slope, with a hedge on the right, to the bottom of a field. Now turn left, still keeping a hedge on the right. Go through a metal gate and keep the same line through two more gates to cross a stream over a plank bridge at a ford. Follow the clear track through gates to reach Park Farm. Cross a cattle grid and continue as far as the pillars of the old railway viaduct.*

3. *The narrow grassy path on the left, immediately before the viaduct, is the start of the return route after retracing steps from Hook Norton. To reach the village, continue to meet a road. Turn left and soon right along Park Road. Swing right over a bridge and climb the alley straight ahead.*

4. *Hook Norton is a large interesting village. As well as a choice of inns, the church, brewery and pottery are worth seeing. Retrace the route back to the path by the viaduct at (3) and follow this path as it passes through two handgates, climbs the embankment, and enters the B.B.O.N.T. nature reserve. Follow the embankment to the left as far as a bridge.*

5. *Climb the steps on the left to reach a road. Turn left and keep on as far as the junction with another road approaching from the right. Continue for 50 metres beyond this junction, then turn left to follow a yellow arrow along a track. Immediately beyond gateposts, turn right down a field, aiming for Swerford church spire. Soon, keep a hedge on the right to reach a road over a stile. Turn right, and in 20 metres, left over another*

stile. Cross a large sloping field, bearing half-left to a stile in a paddock fence, and continue over stiles down two more fields. Cross a stiled footbridge and a low stone bridge and climb to reach a stile, beyond which the route passes through a narrow grassy field planted with trees to strike a track. This climbs to a road. Turn left along it back to Swerford church and the start.

The church, too, is packed with interest. The creatures carved on the font include a man with a horse's body, firing an arrow and a double-headed monster biting itself. Nearby stands the old village fire-engine, a primitive contraption last used in 1896 and now carefully restored. Hook Norton is one of many villages featuring in comical rhymes. According to the local doggerel, it is the place where pigs play the organ - which at least makes a change from the usual derogatory saying about certain villages in which pigs are lifted on to walls to see bands go past!

Refreshments   Choice of inns at Hook Norton.

HIGHLAND CATTLE NEAR DEDDINGTON

Route 13   5½ miles
Deddington and Clifton

Outline Deddington ~ Field Barn ~ Tithe Lane ~ Clifton ~ Leadenporch Farm ~ Chapmans Lane ~ Deddington.

Summary This is an easy walk, chiefly along footpaths, in the valley of the River Cherwell, centred on the ancient market town of Deddington. Deddington lies within a triangle formed by Banbury, Chipping Norton and Bicester, close to the border with Northamptonshire, in gentle country, yet with plenty of colourful historical associations.

Attractions 'Is it a small town or a large village?' Many people visiting Deddington for the first time ask that question. Hardly surprising, because for every feature indicating that this old-world place of rich golden-brown stone deserves to be called a town, there seems to be another suggesting it is in reality merely a village.

As far as its past is concerned, there can be no doubt. Deddington was granted a market in the 13th century and as recently as the last century, the Market Place was the centre of bustling activity, especially on Martinmass Fair day in November. Villagers flocked to town to buy their winter clothes and the streets were cluttered with horses, cattle and sheep, brought for sale from miles around.

In those times, beer was brewed at Deddington and this led to the town being ridiculed in a local rhyme:

'Aynho on the hill, Clifton on the clay,
Drunken Deddington and Hempton Highway'.

Apart from its beer, Deddington had another doubtful claim to fame. This was its pudding pies, made from bread and miscellaneous scraps, encased in suet pastry. The story goes that when a certain king visited the town, the people were uncertain what gift to offer him. Hearing that Woodstock had given him a pair of their famous leather gloves, and that Banbury had presented him with some of their celebrated cakes, the Deddington folk decided on a pudding pie - something as leathery as Woodstock's gift if not quite as edible as Banbury's!

There was once a fine castle at Deddington, in which Piers Gaveston, the vain friend of the discredited King Edward II, was imprisoned by the Earl of Pembroke before being seized by the Earl of Warwick and taken away to face execution at Blacklow Hill, in Warwickshire, in 1312. All that remains of the castle are grassy ramparts and ditches.

continued on page 62

59

Route 13

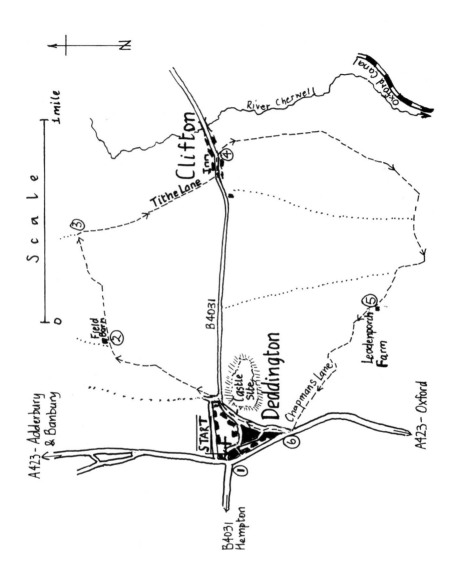

Route 13

Deddington and Clifton

5½ miles

START *Deddington, a small town on the A423 (Banbury-Oxford road). Park in or near the market place. (O.S. Landranger Sheet 151. G.R.466317).*

ROUTE

1. *From the Market Place, walk along Church Street, turning left at a T-junction to reach the B4031. (A diversion can be taken to see the castle site, now a sports field, which is soon signposted on the right). At the junction with Earls Lane on the left, go over a stile (yellow arrow) and cross a field diagonally, passing to the left of a clump of trees to reach another stile in a hedge. Cross another field to a stile by a metal gate and turn left along a concrete road to Field Barn Farm.*

2. *Pass the farm on your left and keep on between barns along a straight farm track. At a T-junction, turn left. When the track swings right, just beyond a fuel tank, follow it down the slope to its junction with Tithe Lane.*

3. *Turn right here and keep straight on to reach the B4031 at Clifton. Turn left into the village. Opposite the Duke of Cumberland's Head, turn right along Chapel Close.*

4. *Beyond the houses, follow the blue bridleway sign, passing a lake on your left. Beyond a metal gate, veer left to follow a hedge along the bottom of a field to reach a handgate. Keep straight on to pass through another handgate with a stream close by. Turn right here but, instead of keeping to the hedge up the slope, veer diagonally left, avoiding the marshy ground, to reach a handgate in a hedge. Continue straight across the next field through a gap in the hedge and keep a hedge on the right as far as a wide green lane, also on the right. Follow this as far as a branch to the left, leading to Leadenporch Farm, with Deddington church visible beyond. Go through a metal gate (yellow arrow) to reach the farm drive.*

5. *Follow the drive, keeping to the left at a fork by a brook before swinging right, opposite poultry sheds. Climb to a stile by a gate and keep on along Chapmans Lane to reach the A423.*

6. *Turn right into Deddington, bearing right again along St. Thomas Street. Pass Goose Green on the left and continue along Philcote Street to reach the Market Place and the start.*

61

Three fine church steeples can be seen to the north of the footpath near Field Barn Farm. Another rhyme describes their contrasting qualities:

'Bloxham for length, Adderbury for strength,
And King's Sutton for beauty'.

Does the old rhyme give a true description of the three differing spires? Please discuss!

To the left of the bridleway leaving Clifton, views can be obtained, not only of the River Cherwell, but also of the Oxford Canal and the railway, both of which were routed along the valley. A glimpse can also be had of a new feature that has made a profound impact on the region - the M40 motorway.

The one farm passed on the return route - Leadenporch Farm - has a varied collection of livestock, including Highland cattle and exotic poultry which, together with seasonal bird and plant life, provides interest all the way back to Deddington.

Refreshments Duke of Cumberland's Head inn, Clifton. Don't be put off by the 'Filthy ale and disgusting food' sign - others aren't!

ALMSHOUSES, CHIPPING NORTON

Route 14   4 miles

Chipping Norton and Salford

Outline   Chipping Norton (New Street car park) ~ Recreation ground-Salford ~ Chipping Norton castle site and church ~ Distons Lane ~ Car park.

Summary   The highest town in Oxfordshire, Chipping Norton stands on a northern spur of the Cotswolds, close to the Gloucestershire border. Set in good walking country, 'Chippy' has a rich history and is well worth a leisurely exploration. Some of the town's leading attractions can be seen on this short walk, along field paths, to the quiet village of Salford. There are a few gentle climbs but nothing really strenuous.

Attractions   After passing through the town's recreation ground, the route climbs over the mouth of the sealed railway tunnel and crosses fields, with good views away westwards towards the Evenlode Valley and Stow-on-the-Wold. Entering Salford, notice the old millstone leaning against a barn at Village Farm. Salford church has a fine carving of a centaur-half-man, half-horse - shown firing an arrow, over its doorway. Inside are two excellently preserved monuments to the Bolter family, dating from the 16th and 17th centuries.

Naturalists in the family may well find the green lane beyond Salford on the return section, the most rewarding part of the walk. The tall hedges on either side are rich in bird life, especially thrushes, blackbirds, chaffinches and yellowhammers. Beyond, as the route passes between wide fields, watch out for lapwings and listen for skylarks rising in full song between March and midsummer. Spotting a soaring skylark at the summit of its climb calls both for patience and a sharp eye.

The return to Chipping Norton is made past the mound of the former castle, long since demolished. To the left of the church, a short way up the steep street, stands a fine row of almshouses, built to accommodate eight poor widows, by Henry Cornish in 1640.

The beautiful 15th century church of St. Mary contains many striking features and is well worth exploring in detail. Two tombstones in the churchyard are especially unusual. One marks the grave of Phillis Humphreys, a rat-catcher's wife, who, the inscription tells us, 'lodged in many a town and travelled far and near'. The other, that of Margaret Taylor, who lived to be 104, records that she lived in three centuries.

Any time remaining can be well spent looking around the town, possibly following the guided trail, a copy of which can be obtained from the Tourist Information Centre on Middle Row. Outstanding features

continued on page 66

E   63

Route 14

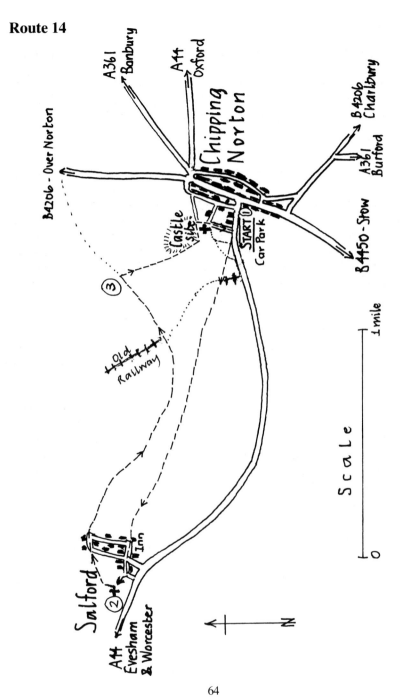

Route 14

Chipping Norton and Salford   4 miles

START   *The car park, New Street, Chipping Norton. The town stands at the junction of the A44 and the A361 and is just over a mile west of the A34. (O.S. Landranger Sheets 163 and 164. G.R.312270).*

ROUTE

1. *From the car park, turn left down New Street. After passing the sign to the museum on the left, enter the recreation ground through a kissing gate. Leave by a similar gate to the left of infants' play apparatus and dip to cross a footbridge. Just beyond, at the foot of the slope, ignore a path to the right. Instead, keep straight on to cross a farm road over two stiles and continue the gentle climb, passing a cemetery on the left. Cross a double stile and keep a hedge on the left to reach another stile at the top left-hand corner of a field. Go straight across the next field towards Salford church, cross a farm track, and descend on the same line to a stile in a hedge gap. Keep a hedge on the left over the next field as far as a stile leading to a grassy track between fences. Follow this to reach a farm. Enter the farmyard through a gate to emerge at Salford. Keep straight on, passing the Black Horse inn on the left, before bearing right to reach the church.*

2. *Walk through the churchyard alongside the right-hand wall and leave through a kissing gate at the far corner. Bear right over a field (yellow arrow) to pass through a hedge gap and reach a road over a stile. Pass a playground on the right and keep straight on past a house called 'Golden', beyond which the route follows a green lane (later a track). At a point where the hedge on the right ends, at a junction of tracks, keep left. Continue past a farm road on the right, as far as a hedge, which descends the field on the right.*

3. *Turn through the gap here, keeping the hedge on the right through a second gap. Approximately half way down the slope, watch for a stile, half hidden in the hedge on the right. From here, the path descends towards Chipping Norton church tower, passing through a kissing gate to reach a shady path. This climbs between the moated castle mound and the churchyard. At the top of the slope, by a sign indicating Pool Meadow, turn sharp right along a footpath through the churchyard, leaving by keeping straight on along the foot of Church Street to arrive back on New Street via Distons Lane. Turn left back to the car park.*

worth searching for include the former British School (dated 1854) on New Street, the solitary pillar - all that remains of the old market hall - by the Victorian town hall, and the White Hart inn, a former coaching inn, well known to travellers bound for London or Worcester, who often broke their journey in the town.

Prominent in the valley south of the town centre is the Bliss Tweed Mill. This was built in 1872 by William Bliss to resemble a country mansion. Tweed cloth was made here until 1980. Nearby stood the old railway station, from which trains on the Oxford, Worcester and Wolverhampton Railway (known locally as The Old Worse and Worse) first linked Chipping Norton with Kingham Junction and Cheltenham in 1855.

Refreshments   Black Horse inn, Salford. Wide choice of inns and cafes in Chipping Norton.

BRIDGE OVER THE EVENLODE

Kingham and the Evenlode Valley

Outline   Kingham ~ Bledington ~ Bledington Heath ~ Oddington
Ashes ~ Kingham.

Summary   The River Evenlode, a tributary of the Thames, flows south
from its source near Moreton-in-Marsh. South of Bledington Heath, it
forms the boundary between Oxfordshire and Gloucestershire.
Kingham, on the Oxfordshire bank, is linked to its neighbour,
Bledington, by a footbridge, and this riverside walk, together with the
meandering bridleway over Bledington Heath (**very** muddy after rain)
and the footpath through Oddington Ashes, makes a flat but challenging
walk with abundant wildlife interest.

Attractions   Kingham is perhaps best known for its railway associations.
It still retains its station on the Hereford-Paddington line but its era of
importance - it was once known as Chipping Norton Junction - has long
since gone. This walk crosses the existing line and also what remains of
the old branch line to Stow-on-the-Wold and Cheltenham. Many stories
are told about this lost line, which wriggled its leisurely way through the
Cotswolds, including one of an engine driver whose locomotive struck
and killed a pheasant. Thinking quickly, he threw his cap on to the line,
entitling him to stop his train on the return journey, and so claim both his
'lost' cap and a good dinner for his family!

Unlike the typical Cotswold rivers - Coln, Dikler, Windrush - the
Evenlode is a reedy sluggish stream of secret pools and muddy depths in
which cattle browse. Crayfish and freshwater mussels once bred
abundantly. Both still lurk unseen in favoured places but walkers are far
more likely to encounter handsome dragonflies and their delicate
relatives, damselflies, both of which breed on the water vegetation.

This vegetation is both varied and colourful, with tall handsome
purple loosestrife contrasting with the bright yellow water lily, known to
country folk as 'Brandy bottle' on account of its smell. By the water's
edge, a host of smaller flowering plants - forget-me-not, brooklime, water
speedwell, among others - add their share of colour.

Bird life provides plenty of interest throughout this walk. The
Evenlode is a kingfisher stream and watchful walkers may well see a flash
of iridescent greenish-blue as one of these peerless birds streaks like an
arrow, low along the water. Failing that, mute swans, herons, mallard
and pied wagtails are all likely to be encountered, while Bledington's
watery village green provides a flotilla of tame, well-fed ducks.

continued on page 70

67

Route 15

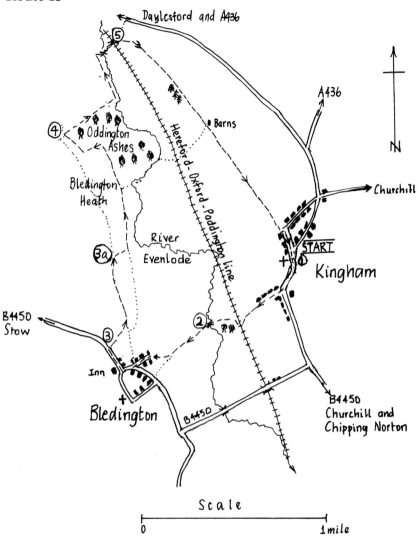

Daylesford and A436

⑤

A436

Barns

④ Oddington
Ashes

Bledington
Heath

Churchill

River
Evenlode

③a

START
① Kingham

B4450
Stow

②

③

Inn

Bledington

B4450

B4450
Churchill and
Chipping Norton

Hereford-Oxford-Paddington line

Scale

0   1 mile

Route 15

Kingham and the Evenlode Valley   5 miles

START   *Kingham, a village between Stow-on-the-Wold and Chipping Norton, reached along minor roads either from the A436 or the B4450. Park in Church Street, as near as possible to the church. (O.S. Landranger Sheet 163. G.R.259238).*

ROUTE

1. *Go through the kissing gate just beyond the lychgate and follow the metalled path. Turn right along a road. When this bends to the left, keep straight on along a path between a lane to houses on the left and gardens on the right. The path leads to a gated crossing over the Paddington-Hereford railway line. Cross with care and turn right, walking parallel to the line for 60 metres, then climb a stile into a field. Aim for the right-hand corner of a low wood on the left, beyond which a footbridge over the River Evenlode links Oxfordshire with Gloucestershire.*

2. *From the bridge, bear half-left to cross an old railway embankment. From here, a stile leads to the footpath to Bledington, which is reached after taking a right fork just beyond a footbridge to reach a stile at the far right-hand corner of a field. Follow a twisting grassy path, which soon becomes a lane, to reach the B4450 at Bledington village green. Leave the village by crossing the road bridge on the right. Beyond the derestriction sign and a bungalow (Orchard Croft), turn right along a bridleway.*

3. *The bridleway crosses the old railway once more and proceeds between hedges for about 1½ miles. (Note: the rutted surface can be **very** muddy after rain. In these conditions, it is recommended that families with young children leave the bridleway at (3a) and follow the public footpath (dotted line on map) on its roughly parallel course to link up with the route at (4).*

4. *The route leaves the bridleway in woodland (Oddington Ashes), just before a marker post on the left, at a right-hand bend. Turn right into the wood along a wide track, roughly surfaced at first. This narrows eventually into a woodland path. At the end of the wood, follow the yellow arrow to the left. Daylesford church spire can be seen straight ahead. Keep a hedge, and the Evenlode, on the right as far as a footbridge. Cross this and, in a short distance, cross the gated bridge over the railway.*

5. *Immediately beyond the second gate, cross a field diagonally to the right to a field gate. Beyond, keep a hedge on the left, passing first a conifer wood and then large barns. From here, a clear farm road leads back to Kingham. After passing houses, turn left at a T-junction by a lime tree and then right to reach another T-junction. The church is on the right.*

The dense woodland of Oddington Ashes offers contrasting wildlife watching. Contrary to its name, this wood is a mixture of ash and oak, with a variety of other species comprising a lower storey. This makes for a rich plant population and provides habitat for such tree-loving birds as great-spotted woodpecker, coal tit and sparrow hawk. Speckled wood, ringlet and gatekeeper butterflies haunt the woodland glades during the summer months.

Refreshments King's Head, Bledington. Children's playground adjoining.

WIDFORD CHURCH

Route 16

(or 2¼ miles omitting Handley Plain)

Swinbrook and Widford

Outline   Swinbrook ~ Widford church ~ Widford Manor ~ Blacksmith Lane ~ Handley Plain ~ Dean Bottom ~ Swinbrook.

Summary   The lovely Windrush becomes an Oxfordshire river a couple of miles west of Burford and this corner of the county is arguably its finest portion of the Cotswolds. The little wool town of Burford is of course packed with good things, while for those families who wish to combine a visit with a short easy country walk, Swinbrook and Widford await. Here, in the space of little more than two miles, are to be found abundant history, architecture, folklore, wildlife -all the ingredients, in fact, to make a memorable experience.

Attractions   Swinbrook, standing on a slope above the River Windrush, was once owned by a family called Fettiplace, people so wealthy that they featured in a well-known Cotswold chant:
'The Traceys, the Lacys and the Fettiplaces,
Own all the woods, the parks and the chases'.
Like their mansion, which stood to the south-west of the church, the Fettiplaces have long since gone. However, in the church can be seen their effigies - six Fettiplaces, finely carved, resting on their elbows on a tiered monument, which gives the impression, as one young visitor remarked, that they are stacked in bunk beds. They seem so lifelike that one writer described them as looking 'as if they were ready to spring up into life at a moment's notice, and only waited for the signal'.
After the departure of the Fettiplaces, their fine old house was let to a Mr. Freeman of London, a young man with an extravagant life-style, who brought his own servants with him. At about this time, a series of highway robberies took place in the vicinity and on one of these, a coach guard shot dead one of the raiders, who proved to be Mr. Freeman's butler. Enquiries followed, and 'Mr. Freeman' was identified as a notorious and much-wanted highwayman!
Widford church stands alone in the fields, the village it once served now only a few mounds scarcely visible on the sloping field close by. Inside this little church is a most unusual sight - a fragment of Roman mosaic embedded in the floor of the chancel and evidence that the 12th century builders chose to erect their church on the remains of a Roman building, possibly a villa.   *continued on page 72*

71

Route 16

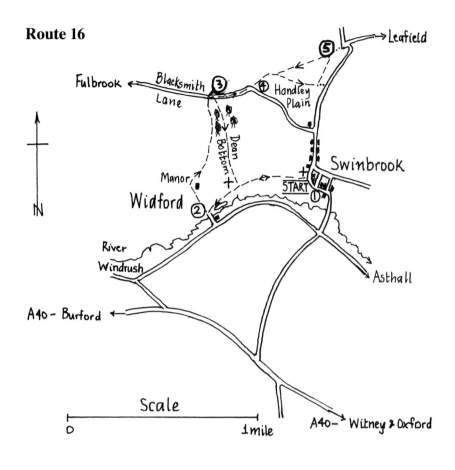

Beyond the church, a lake on the left offers bird-watching possibilities, with mute swans, coots, moorhens and mallard usually present.

Further on, at the top of a drive, stands Widford Manor, a grand old house of Cotswold stone that so inspired the folk-lore writer Katherine M. Briggs that she wrote a children's story, 'Hobberdy Dick', set within its ancient walls at the time of the Civil War. Dick was a kindly spirit who had 'lived' in the old house for many years and was determined that its insensitive new owner should not destroy its age-old atmosphere - a good read.

Refreshments Maytime Inn, Asthall (1 mile S.W. of Swinbrook).

Route 16

Swinbrook and Widford

3½ miles

(or 2¼ miles omitting Handley Plain)

START   *Swinbrook. The village lies midway between the A361 and the A40, 2 miles east of Burford, from which it can be approached along a minor road, Witney Street, midway up the Hill. In Swinbrook, park by the little green below the church (O.S. Landranger Sheet 163. G.R.281122).*

ROUTE

1. *From the green, cross the road and take the pebbly path past the postbox. This soon becomes a footpath between stone walls before entering fields through a handgate. Widford church now comes into view ahead. Cross a stile and pass a footpath sign indicating a path to the right (the return route). The church may be visited now or later. Beyond it, follow the straight track to reach the drive to Widford Manor.*

2. *Turn right and climb past the Manor to reach a metal gate (blue arrow). Follow the bridleway, which soon swings to the right. Keep a hedge, then woodland, on the right, as far as a road (Blacksmith Lane).*

3. *Turn right. (Those wishing to follow the shorter route should turn right again over a stile in 30 metres). Otherwise, keep on along the road as far as a bridleway (blue arrow) on the left at a right-hand bend.*

4. *Follow the bridleway down to a gate. 20 metres beyond, leave the track and go through a gap in the wall on the right. Keep on along the left flank of a tiny valley, passing springs on the right. Cross two stiles. Beyond the second, climb the bank, keeping first a hedge, then a wall, on the right, to reach the bridleway once more.*

5. *Turn left to pass through the gate again and climb to the road. Turn right and retrace to the stile mentioned for the shorter route. Follow the footpath between woods into Dean Bottom. Cross the stile near Widford church and turn left to retrace the outward route back to Swinbrook, making a slight diversion by going through the white gate by the cottage at the end of the walled footpath to pass through the churchyard.*

Appendices

ROUTES IN ORDER OF DIFFICULTY

Easy short walks
Route 2 — *Wilmcote and the Stratford Canal*
Route 3 — *Round about Napton-on-the-Hill*
Route 16 — *Swinbrook and Widford*

More strenuous walks *(less than 5 miles)*
Route 5 — *Round about Wormleighton*
Route 9 — *Ilmington Downs*
Route 11 — *Around and about Swalcliffe*
Route 14 — *Chipping Norton and Salford*

Easy longer walks *(5 or more miles)*
Route 1 — *Alcester and the Arrow Valley*
Route 4 — *Grand Union and Oxford Canals*
Route 10 — *Brailes Country*
Route 12 — *Swerford and Hook Norton*
Route 13 — *Deddington and Clifton*

More strenuous longer walks *(5 or more miles)*
Route 6 — *Warmington, Ratley and Hornton*
Route 7 — *Cropredy, Wardington and the Oxford Canal*
Route 8 — *Meon Hill*
Route 15 — *Kingham and the Evenlode Valley*

PUBLIC TRANSPORT

Although a good many of the walking routes included in this book are in somewhat remote rural areas, most can be reached by public transport. As both train and bus timetables are subject to seasonal and other changes, sometimes at short notice, families are advised to check with rail and bus operators to ensure that they have up-to-date timetables.

Alternatively, these times can be verified at one of the Tourist Information Centres listed on the appropriate page. T.I.C.s carry copies of timetables and will advise on route planning and other related matters.

Oxfordshire County Council, in conjunction with the Connection Publishing Co. Ltd., issue an excellent publication called 'Connections', which is regularly updated and which includes complete details of rail and bus services in the Banbury area. This can be obtained free of charge from Banbury Tourist Information Centre or direct from the publishers (Tel. 0844 274349).

Other useful addresses and telephone numbers:
Rail services, Stratford area .... Tel. 0203 555211
              Banbury area .... Tel. 0494 441561
Bus services, Stratford area .... Tel. 0788 535555 — Stratford Blue
              Banbury area .... Tel. 0295 262368 — Midland Red
                                  Tel. 021 622 4373 — National Express

Rural bus service operators

Brailes Coaches	Tel. 060 885 243
Catteralls Coach & Travel Services (Southam)	Tel. 092 681 3840
Geoff Amos Coaches Ltd. (East of Banbury)	Tel. 0327 60522
Heyfordian Travel Ltd. (South of Banbury)	Tel. 0869 232957
Oxford Bus Company	Tel. 0865 711312
David R. Grasby Coach Hire (Edgehill area)	Tel. 0926 640455
Hedgehog Community Bus (Stratford - C. Campden)	Tel. 0452 425543

MUSEUMS — Warwickshire

Edgehill Battle Museum, Farnborough Hall, nr. Banbury.
Leamington Art Gallery & Museum, Avenue Road, Leamington Spa.
Napton Nickleodeon, High Street, Napton-on-the-Hill.
Ashorne Nickleodeon Collection, Ashorne Hill, nr. Warwick.
Stratford Motor Museum, Shakespeare Street, Stratford-on-Avon.
Teddy Bear Museum, 19 Greenhill Street, Stratford-on-Avon.
Warwickshire Museum, Market Place, Warwick.
Warwickshire Doll Museum, Oken's House, Castle Street, Warwick.
Royal Warwickshire Regimental Museum, St. John's House, Warwick.
St. John's House Museum, St. John's, Warwick.
Midland Air Museum, Coventry Airport, Baginton.
Lunt Roman Fort, Baginton.
The World of Shakespeare, Waterside, Stratford-on-Avon.
Shakespeare's Birthplace, Henley Street, Stratford-on-Avon.
New Place/Nash's House, Chapel Street, Stratford-on-Avon.
Hall's Croft, Old Town, Stratford-on-Avon.
Ann Hathaway's Cottage, Shottery, nr. Stratford-on-Avon.
Mary Arden's House & Shakespeare Countryside Museum, Wilmcote.

MUSEUMS — Oxfordshire

Banbury Museum, 8 Horsefair.
Bloxham Village Museum, The Court House, Bloxham.
Granary Museum, Butlin Farm, Claydon, nr. Banbury.
Swalcliffe Great Barn, nr. Banbury.
Tolsey Museum, Burford.
Cogges Manor Farm Museum, nr. Witney.
Chipping Norton Museum.

HISTORIC BUILDINGS — Warwickshire

Ragley Hall, nr. Alcester.
Charlecote Park, nr. Wellesbourne.
Wellesbourne Water Mill, Mill Farm, Kineton Road, Wellesbourne.
Coughton Court, nr. Alcester.
Warwick Castle.
Kenilworth Castle.
Upton House, nr. Banbury.
Farnborough Hall, nr. Banbury.

HISTORIC BUILDINGS — Oxfordshire
Broughton Castle, nr. Banbury.
Minster Lovell Hall and Dovecote, Minster Lovell, nr. Witney.
North Leigh Roman Villa nr. Witney.
Wroxton Abbey House and Gardens, nr. Banbury.

OTHER PLACES OF INTEREST — Warwickshire
Burton Dassett Country Park, nr. Kineton.
Brass Rubbing Centre, Avonbank Gardens, Stratford-on-Avon.
Chesterton Windmill, nr. Harbury.
Butterfly and Jungle Safari, The Tramway, Stratford-on-Avon.
Shire Horse Centre and Farm Park, Clifford Road, Stratford-on-Avon.
Southam Zoo, Daventry Road, Southam.
Kinwarton Dovecote, nr. Alcester.

OTHER PLACES OF INTEREST — Oxfordshire
Waterfowl Sanctuary, Wigginton Heath, nr. Banbury.
Adderbury Lakes Nature Reserve, nr. Banbury.
Hook Norton Railway Nature Reserve, nr. Banbury.
The Rollright Stones, Prehistoric Monument, nr. Chipping Norton.
Cotswold Wildlife Park, nr. Burford.

USEFUL ADDRESSES AND INFORMATION

TOURIST INFORMATION CENTRES — Warwickshire
Stratford-on-Avon, Bridgefoot, Stratford-on-Avon. Tel. (0789) 293127.
Leamington Spa, Jephson Lodge, The Parade. Tel. (0926) 311470.
Warwick, The Court House, Jury Street. Tel. (0926) 492212.

TOURIST INFORMATION CENTRES — Oxfordshire
Oxford, St. Aldates. Tel. (0865) 726873.
Banbury, The Museum, 8 Horsefair. Tel. (0295) 259855.
Burford, The Brewery, Sheep Street. Tel. (099382) 3558.
Chipping Norton, Middle Row. Tel. (0608) 644379.
Cropredy, The Wharf, Cropredy, Banbury. Tel. (029575) 8203.
Witney, Cogges Farm Museum, Church Lane, Cogges. Tel. (0993) 72602.
Woodstock, The Library, Hensington Road. Tel. (0993) 811038.
Advice on countryside access matters:
General
The Ramblers Association, 1/5 Wandsworth Road, London. SW8 2XX.
Warwickshire
The Country Services Dept., Warwickshire County Council, Shire Hall, Warwick.
Oxfordshire
The Countryside Services Dept., Oxfordshire County Council, Library Service Headquarters, Holton, Oxford. OX9 1QQ.
Nature Conservation
Warwickshire
The Warwickshire Nature Conservation Trust, Montague Road, Warwick. CV34 5LW.
Oxfordshire
The Berks, Bucks & Oxon Naturalists' Trust, 3 Church Cowley Road, Oxford. OX4 3JR.

BACKGROUND READING ON THE AREA

Warwickshire
Warwickshire Villages, Lyndon F. Cave, Hale.
Warwickshire, Douglas Hickman, Faber and Faber.
The Warwickshire Village Book, Warwicks. Fed. W.I. & Countryside Books.
Hidden Warwickshire, Betty Smith, Countryside Books.
Warwickshire (King's England Series), Ed. A. Mee., Hodder & Stoughton.
Warwickshire, F. R. Banks, Penguin.
Warwickshire, Alan Burgess, Hale.

Oxfordshire
Portrait of Oxfordshire, Christine Bloxham, Hale.
Oxfordshire, Reginald Turnor, Elek.
Oxfordshire and Oxford, Marilyn Yurdan, Shire Publications.
Companion into Oxfordshire, E. C. Williams, Methuen.
Oxfordshire, Joanna Cannan, Hale.
Oxfordshire, (King's England Series) Ed. A. Mee, Hodder & Stoughton.
The Oxfordshire Village Book, Oxon, Fed. W.I. & Countryside Books.

General
Visitor's Guide to the Severn and Avon, Lawrence Garner, Moorland.
The Centre of England, Victor Skipp, Eyre Methuen.
The English Heartland, R. & M. Beckinsale, Duckworth.
The Folklore of the Cotswolds, Katherine M. Briggs, Batsford.
Discovering Canals, Metcalfe and Vince, Shire Publications.

STRATFORD CANAL (Route 2)

77

FAMILY WALKS SERIES

Family Walks in the North Yorkshire Dales. Howard Beck. ISBN 0 907758 52 5.

Family Walks in West Yorkshire. Howard Beck. ISBN 0 907758 43 6.

Family Walks in Three Peaks and Malham. Howard Beck. ISBN 0 907758 42 8.

Family Walks in South Yorkshire. Norman Taylor. ISBN 0 907758 25 8.

Family Walks in the North Wales Borderlands. Gordon Emery. ISBN 0 907758 50 9.

Family Walks in Cheshire. Chris Buckland. ISBN 0 907758 29 0.

Family Walks in the Staffordshire Peak and Potteries. Les Lumsdon. ISBN 0 907758 34 7.

Family Walks in the White Peak. Norman Taylor. ISBN 0 907758 09 6.

Family Walks in the Dark Peak. Norman Taylor. ISBN 0 907758 16 9.

Family Walks in Snowdonia. Laurence Main. ISBN 0 907758 32 0.

Family Walks in Mid Wales. Laurence Main. ISBN 0 907758 27 4.

Family Walks in South Shropshire. Marian Newton. ISBN 0 907758 30 4.

Family Walks in the Teme Valley. Camilla Harrison. ISBN 0 907758 45 2.

Family Walks in Hereford and Worcester. Gordon Ottewell. ISBN 0 907758 20 7.

Family Walks around Cardiff and the Valleys. Gordon Hindess. ISBN 0 907758 54 1.

Family Walks in the Wye Valley. Heather and Jon Hurley. ISBN 0 907758 26 6.

Family Walks in Warwickshire. Geoff Allen. ISBN 0 907758 53 3.

Family Walks around Stratford and Banbury. Gordon Ottewell. ISBN 0 907758 49 5.

Family Walks in the Cotswolds. Gordon Ottewell. ISBN 0 907758 15 0.

Family Walks in South Gloucestershire. Gordon Ottewell. ISBN 0 907758 33 9.

Family Walks in Oxfordshire. Laurence Main. ISBN 0 907758 38 X.

Family Walks around Bristol, Bath and the Mendips. Nigel Vile. ISBN 0 907758 19 3.

Family Walks in Wiltshire. Nigel Vile. ISBN 0 907758 21 5.

Family Walks in Berkshire and North Hampshire. Kathy Sharp. ISBN 0 907758 37 1.

Family Walks on Exmoor and the Quantocks John Caswell. ISBN 0 907758 46 0.

Family Walks in Mendip, Avalon and Sedgemoor. Nigel Vile. ISBN 0 907758 41 X.

Family Walks in Cornwall. John Caswell. ISBN 0 907758 55 X.

Family Walks on the Isle of Wight. Laurence Main. ISBN 0 907758 56 8.

Family Walks in North West Kent. Clive Cutter. ISBN 0 907758 36 3.

Family Walks in the Weald of Kent and Sussex. Clive and Sally Cutter. ISBN 0 907758 51 7.

The Publishers, D. J. Mitchell and E. G. Power welcome suggestions for further titles in this Series; and will be pleased to consider manuscripts relating to Derbyshire from new or established authors.
